Harald Haarmann & LaBGC

Illuminating the legacy of Marija Gimbutas –

Old Europe's far-reaching trail in light
of its cultural continuity

Table of contents

Introduction: Old Europe and its cultural heritage in focus 1

1. The cultural fabric of Old Europe and the issue of continuity 8
   – The subsequent cultures as 'daughters' of Old Europe: Minoan, Cycladic, Pelasgian 11
   – The emergence of Greek culture as an Indo-European/Old European amalgamation 17
   – Reflections of the Old European heritage in nowadays national cultures of southeastern Europe 16

2. Foundations of Old European worldview and the imprint on cultural self-awareness 19

3. Communality and the issue of egalitarianism 23
   – Economic egalitarianism 26
   – Social egalitarianism 30

4. Focusing on a female divinity: The heiresses of the Great Goddess 35

5. Old European goddesses as patrons of Indo-European heroes 43

6. The spirit of Olympia: The resurrection of an Old European institution 52

7. The Neolithic spirit in art and its timeless aesthetic appeal 60

8. The Danube script (c. 5500 – c. 2600 BCE): Sign inventory, social functions and derivations .. 68

9. Origins of theater as performative art 77
   – The Old European tradition of theater as performance 79
   – The Greek innovation of theater as architectural form 81

10. The Odyssey: Old European soundings in world literature 84
    – Odysseus and his patron Athena: An intimate companionship 90
    – The topic of peace as common good 91

11. Seafaring and shipbuilding: The longevity of Old European expertise 94

12. The hexameter and its pre-Greek origin 100

13. The findings of Marija Gimbutas focusing on migration – Contours of a differential typology 104
    – Multifaceted motivations for migration 107

- Conditions for migration motivated by intentions to control a lucrative trade market (Kurgan I) 111
- Conditions for migration triggering the second out-migration (Kurgan II) 120
- Conditions for migration facilitated by the introduction of wheel and wagon (Kurgan III) 128
- The input of ancient European technology and the fabric of ancient European terminology 131
- Conclusion 133

Epilog: Mission to finally integrate Old Europe into historiography 134

Bibliography i

List of maps and figures xx
    Maps xx
    Figures xxi

Motto
- "[…] the Old European sacred images and symbols were never totally uprooted; these most persistent features in human history were too deeply implanted in the psyche." (Gimbutas 1989: 318)

Introduction:
Old Europe and its cultural heritage in focus

It is the great merit of Marija Gimbutas (1921-1994) to have highlighted the contours of the Old European advanced society, conceived as a blanket term overarching several regional cultures in southeastern Europe – Vinča, Turdaș and Tărtăria, Karanovo, Cucuteni, Gumelnița, Trypillya – their egalitarian economic and communal life. She inspired imagination with the descriptions of a worldview focusing on a female divinity, with expressions in art, a complex system of signs and symbols and early technological achievements. Moreover, she outlined Old European influence into all directions. Marija Gimbutas elaborated a thorough documentation of how the traditions of these peacefully prospering societies were overformed with hierarchy and patriarchy by immigrating Indo-Europeans from the steppe. This eminent scholar's discovery is an essential ingredient in humankind's history and her insights are of an exceptional magnitude for the humanities (Marler 2022a, 2022b).

The findings of Marija Gimbutas have enriched and invigorated studies and scientific exchange among the different disciplines – archaeology, ancient history, linguistics, sociology, comparative religion and art. In a way, building on the legacy of Marija Gimbutas became a mission. The great panorama of ancient Europe and its structure gained in profile.

For a long time Marija Gimbutas's fieldwork on Old Europe as an ancient civilization was debated. Findings have been doubted and discredited. Unjustly, so. The results of subsequent research confirmed her work and today there is consensus among experts that Old Europe is the so far oldest known advanced culture of humankind.

Nevertheless, ignorant of scientific development those who are still following their accustomed canon of traditional civilization research continue to associate Mesopotamia with the notion of *ex oriente lux* ("light from the East") and consider the Middle East to be the "cradle of civilization". At the time when Marija Gimbutas was conducting her research, this view was quite understandable, since many results had not yet been confirmed by additional studies. Findings from interdisciplinary research that lead to the revision of data previously considered secure are continuously reconfirmed in recent studies, and new insights call for a significant revision not only of historiography but for various scientific fields of the humanities.

Ever new discoveries are adding to the validity of Old Europe as advocated by Marija Gimbutas, and the documentation and dating of material evidence have been secured with new dating methods. Thus, the chronological sequence of the Old European cultural horizon has been mapped out and its validity reconfirmed. High time to correct outdated knowledge, to disseminate the valid findings about the first advanced civilization of mankind, its marks in subsequent cultures with influence up to the present, in words and images and, eventually bringing about a corrective of the related historiography.

Just to illustrate the foregoing: According to the canon of *ex oriente lux* Mesopotamia and its early Sumerian civilization were credited for the development of early urbanized settlements and of urban life-ways, for the introduction of the plough and the potter's wheel, for the early smelting of metal, for the first use of writing numbers and writing language. Mesopotamia is also credited for the invention of wheel and wagon. But none of these innovations originated in Mesopotamia. All this and a series of impressive developments originated in Old Europe:

– The world's first use of the plough;

– The world's first advanced culture – and this with egalitarian organization;

– The world's first urban agglomerations (the mega-settlements of the Copper Age in Old Europe emerged hundreds of years earlier than the first Sumerian cities of Mesopotamia);

– The world's first wide trading network, stretching for thousands of kilometers and connecting hundreds of settlements (river trade, sea-borne trade);

– The world's first two-storey buildings and condominiums;

– The world's first sign system for writing numbers;

– The world's first writing;

– The invention of the potter's wheel (first documented for the area of the eastern Cucuteni-Trypillya culture);

- The invention of the two-storey furnace with an upper chamber for burning ceramic ware and a lower chamber for heating;
- The smelting of copper (beginnings around 5400 BCE in southern Serbia);
- The working of gold (the world's oldest artifacts made of gold from Varna in Bulgaria, dating to c. 4500 BCE);
- The world's first wheel technology as a breakthrough development in cooperation with Indo-European pastoralists on the eastern fringe of Old Europe, in the area of modern-day Moldova and western Ukraine. The timeframe for the advancement of wheel technology was the span between the end of the second immigration of Indo-Europeans from the Eurasian steppe in nowadays Russia and Ukraine (Kurgan II) around 3800 BCE and the beginning of the third immigration (Kurgan III) around 3200 BCE.

The basic terminology of this technology is of Indo-European coinage while a more specialized set of technical terms is related to the non-Indo-European language of the ancient Europeans. Elements of this specialized terminology for wheel and wagon persisted, as lexical borrowings, in the vocabulary of ancient Greek (Haarmann 2022).

The Palaeolithic and Mesolithic Europeans had been hunter-gatherers until they found out the advantages of a sedentary life with herding small animals such as sheep and goats and farming. In the coastal region of southern Europe (in the historical landscape of Thessaly in nowadays Greece) this change developed amidst a milieu of sociocultural contacts with pioneer groups of Anatolian farmers as has been specified by gene analysis. The former hunter-gatherers experienced a process of acculturation, and around 6000 BCE the agrarian lifeway that spread inland into southeastern Europe proved itself useful and beneficial for a peaceful egalitarian coexistence. That was the background for the emergence of Old Europe as the earliest model of a commonwealth in human history.

> "Differences in geo-cultural records combined with DNA databank from prehistoric Europe suggest that local foragers, hunter-gatherers and herders in certain parts of the Balkans could have also initiated farming independently and/or adopted it from farmers they interacted." (Yakar 2016: 30)

The regions where Old European civilization – also known as Danube civilization – once flourished and where path-breaking discoveries were made encompass all of modern-day Hungary, Croatia, Kosovo, Albania, Bosnia-Herzegovina, Serbia, Montenegro, Northern Macedonia, Greece, Bulgaria, Romania, Moldova, and western Ukraine. Here, according to today's knowledge people had developed their togetherness into the first advanced civilization (civilization in the sense of high culture) by building up on the experience of traditions and rules that had ensured coexistence and survival of their Palaeoltihic ancestors for centuries. In this advance civilization people prospered in this vast area for some 3000 years, without experiencing armed conflict and destruction; they were enormously creative and productive, exchanging goods, ideas and innovations with neighboring settlements and in trade with far away regions. Trade routes took them as far as the Atlantic Ocean in the West, Southern England, the present Baltic States, the steppes of Russia, Anatolia and Northern Africa, which in turn were incorporated into the network of contacts. A trading cycle, to which all contributed responsibly, and from which everyone benefitted.

This ensemble of agrarian lifeway, cultural advancement with gender equality and an orientation at the common good became a hub of exchanges, of information, technology, creativity, world views, languages, and collaborations of all kinds (map 1).

Map 1: The network of local and interregional trade routes inside and outside the core area of Old Europe

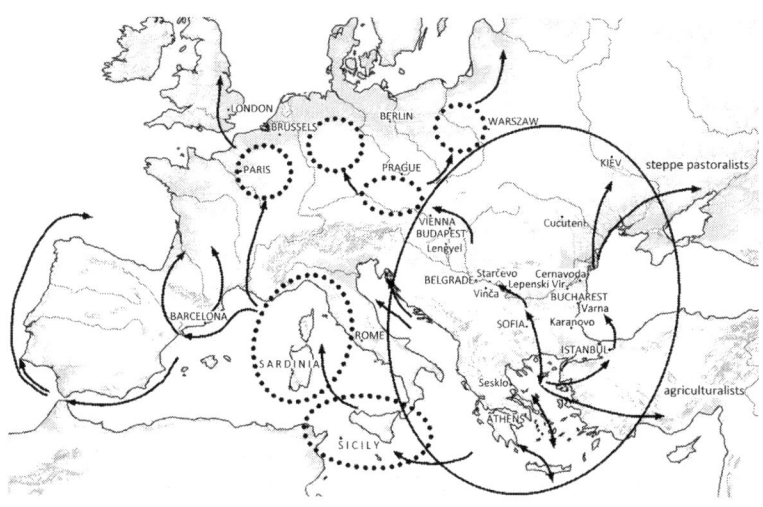

(Haarmann 2020a: 62)

Given the geographical extension of these trade routes it does not seem farfetched to address the Old European trading network as the antecedent of the modern economic zone within the borders of the European Union.

In a comparative outline of the panorama of ancient civilizations, the cultural horizon and the favourable conditions of Old Europe for the development of its plethora of first achievements has been highlighted (Haarmann 2020a). An essay contemplating on our togetherness mirrors the ancient European system of coexistence in towns, villages and on trade routes into our own time (LaBGC & Haarmann 2019; English version 2021).

It is the great merit of Marija Gimbutas to have set the organic whole of Old European structures in perspective. Without her view on the overarching elements the cultural achievements and the technological innovations in southeastern Europe could have been mistaken for random developments lacking a network of internal interconnections. Her work has opened the view on the concerted emergence of this ancient civilization and has inspired interdisciplinary research.

1. The cultural fabric of Old Europe and the issue of continuity

From November 2009 to April 2010, a big exhibition was organized in New York, focusing on Old Europe: *The lost world of Old Europe – The Danube valley, 5000-3500 BC*, with an accompanying exhibition catalogue edited by David W. Anthony (2010). The visitors showed themselves impressed by the wealth of exhibits reflecting the high standards of this advanced culture. And some may have left the exhibition with a sense of regret that the civilization that once flourished in southeastern Europe had vanished without leaving any significant traces. The title of the exhibition had suggested that. Yet, this was unfortunate.

Marija Gimbutas, in her perception of Old Europe and its lasting values, had pointed out trails of cultural continuity, with connections into subsequent cultures. Those inspired by Marija Gimbutas have picked up the threads of her visionary research and have intensified scientific investigation of the fusion processes between the Old European and the Indo-European society and how certain ingredients persisted into later eras. In recent years, many significant discoveries have been made, illuminating the manifold ways in which the Old European heritage has proven its longevity – and this not only in the regional cultures of southeastern Europe. An important link in the chronological sequence from Old Europe into subsequent cultures is its echo from the pre-Indo-European civilization on Greek soil. The emergence of Greek culture – the Greeks being descendants of Indo-Europeans – dates to the late third millennium BCE and its fabric is an agglomerate of Old European and Indo-European features.

To understand the impact, it is necessary to imagine the progression of the fusion process. Due to trade contacts of ancient Europeans with pastoral Indo-Europeans there had not been problems with each other for a long time. It was not until about 4600/4500 BCE that they began to come into conflict in the north east with a first small out-migration (Kurgan I) from the steppe, clashed with the second (Kurgan II) which advanced further into Old European territory around 3500 BCE and with the third and biggest wave of migration around 3000-2800 BCE (Kurgan III) that was fatal for the integrity of Old European culture (see Haarmann & LaBGC 2021 for an outline). Marija Gimbutas, asked in 1989 about her excavations in Old Europe, expressed her deep concerns in the following way (see also installation WAKE UP, p 137):

> "Weapons, weapons weapons! It's just incredible how many thousands of pounds of these daggers and swords were found from the Bronze Age. This was a cruel period and the beginning of what it is today – you turn on the television, and it's war, war, war, whatever channel."

By 2800 BCE Indo-Europeans had infiltrated into most of southeastern Europe and came to dominate the major areas of Old Europe (Gimbutas 1991: 351 ff., Anthony 2007: 225 ff., Haarmann 2012: 87 ff.). By then the Old European cooperative society following the principle of gender equality was syncretizised by the Indo-European culture of patriarchal and possession orientated values.

Yet, the traditions from the old era were not eradicated completely. Under Indo-European aegis traditions that fittet the new system continued, experiencing transformations in the fusion processes and some even survived altogether, even though already around 3500 BCE, the cultural exchange had left traces: "(…) an amalgamation of the Old European and Kurgan cultural systems is clearly evident" (Gimbutas 1991: 371). Further traces of continuity can be found in the wide trade network throughout Europe and especially in regions to which Old European groups migrated after Kurgan I, II and III, and where they later merged with the system of Indo-Europeans, who spread successively in all directions.

In this way the cultural heritage of Old Europe left its imprint in subsequent cultures over a wide geographical area, extending beyond the geographical boundaries of south-eastern Europe. It ranges from nowadays Vienna to Kiev, from southern Poland to the island of Crete in the Aegean Sea. In a wider perspective, continuity of Old European patterns and features can be generally identified in the cultures of our western civilization, mostly transferred through the medium of Greek culture and language which became themselves heavily infused with the ancient pre-Indo-European heritage (see below).

- **The subsequent cultures as 'daughters' of Old Europe: Minoan, Cycladic, Pelasgian**

The selective transformation of Old European traditions into insular (i.e. Aegean) and continental (i.e. Pelasgian) patterns was a process of an repetitive continuity of pertinent features of the pre-Indo-European culture, rather than a fragmentization of the original entity in the sense that, after Kurgan I, II and III the Old-European canon repeated itself in the Aegean civilizations and on the mainland, and its major characteristics continued to be significant. The vivid continuity of Old European features in later periods (i.e. the Aegean Bronze Age) has given raise to the idea that the Minoan civilization of ancient Crete (third and second millennia BCE) and the Pelasgian culture on the continent (second millennium BCE) can be perceived as daughters of the Old European mother culture.

There is evidence that Old European customs continued, and this is true for some communal processes, for the memory of religious imagery as well as for linear signs and their former use that was kept alive by indigenous ancient Europeans in southern Greece. This can be concluded from the finds of two categories of leitmotif in the archaeological record from the Early Helladic II (2500-2200 BCE) and Early Helladic III periods (2200-2000 BCE), and these are terracotta figurines (figure 1a) and linear signs on seals (figure 1b) and on pottery.

Figure 1: The continuation of Old European leitmotifs

a) A figurine from Lerna

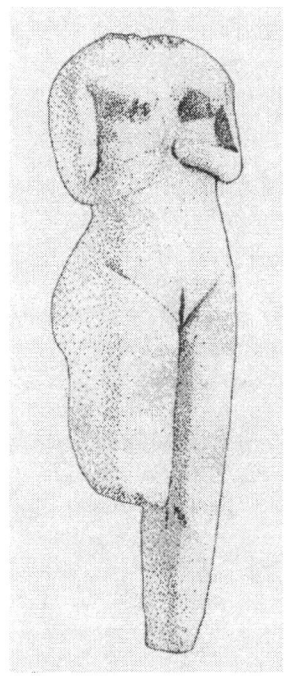

(Runnels and Murray 2001: 58)

b) Clay seals with linear signs from Lerna

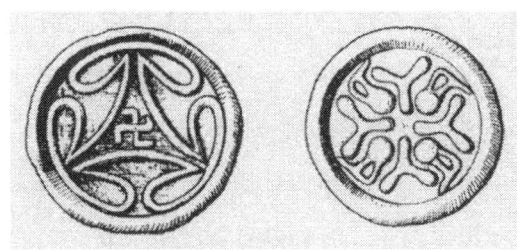

(Dickinson 1994: 190)

- **The emergence of Greek culture as an Indo-European/Old European amalgamation**

As we know, the Greeks are not indigenous to the land that came to be called Hellas in antiquity. Their ancestors, Indo-European pastoralists, after migrating from the steppe into the northern Balkan extended their presence Balkans into Greece in the course of the third millennium BCE (Anthony 2007: 361 ff.). Here as in the Balkans – Greece and the Balkans by then Old European territory – the newcomers encountered the indigenous Old Europeans (descendants of the Palaeo-Europeans) whose culture and language differed markedly from the newcomers, later known as Greeks (descendants of Indo-Europeans). As to the language of the ancient Europeans it has been clarified that "pre-Greek is non-Indo-European" (Beekes 2010: xlii). The Indo-European migrants merged with the local population. Many generations later, in a milieu of culture and language contacts, the tribal profile of the Greek *ethnos* consolidated that we know from antiquity (Haarmann 2013b).

The continuity of Old European elements in this is anchored in a variety of domains, of communal and material culture as well as in spiritual conceptualizations. Key technologies of crafts such as pottery, metallurgy, architecture, ship-building and others were adopted by the Greeks together with pertinent elements of their terminologies (see Haarmann 2014 for a survey).

Interaction between the two (ethnically distinct) groups, indigenous ancient Europeans and Indo-European migrants settling in Hellas, resulted in a prolonged process of fusion when the cultural traditions, the linguistic systems and mythologies in experienced contact-induced interferences. This fusion process can be reconstructed for Pelasgian-Greek contacts, for boundary-crossing of linguistic systems and for "the hybridization of two very different culture systems" (Gimbutas 1991: 401).

The newcomers absorbed much of the knowledge of the Old European population and the impact of the culture of the ancients on Greek civilization became manifested in the transfer of advanced technologies and of markers of high culture (Haarmann 2013a, 2014, 2017).

Greek civilization offers a kaleidoscope of facets of fusion, of pre-Greek elements with Greek items in various fields of culture and in a broad layer of borrowings, from the substrate language, in the vocabulary of ancient Greek. The number of pre-Greek lexical elements exceeds 2,000 (Haarmann 2014: 50 ff.). This inventory includes some 1,700 expressions in general use and also items of specialized terminologies as well as several hundred names (i.e. names of persons and places). These pre-Greek elements are not simply scattered, as single and isolated expressions, throughout the lexicon of ancient Greek. Instead, they are interrelated through their meanings and form part of terminological networks by which cultural domains distinguish and individualize themselves.

The Greeks assimilated many expressions associated with the arts and crafts, in the process of their adoption. Those borrowed terms of pre-Greek origin were integrated in the lexical structures of ancient Greek and, in Greek transformation, they even remained in the cultural vocabulary of our modern languages. Among those linguistic indicators of the Old European substratum are well-known terms, belonging to various domains, such as anchor, aroma, olive and wine (cultivation), ceramics, chemistry, chimney, metal, hymn, lyre, myth, psyche, and others.

What happened in southeastern Europe in the third and second millennia BCE may be compared to what happened thousands of years later in the same region. In the first century BCE, the Romans conquered Greece and the Balkanic region. But Greek culture of antiquity influenced Roman culture to a decisive degree. In other words: those who had been conquered by the force of arms conquered the conqueror by the impact of their culture. And in all the mergers, elements of the Old European culture continued.

- **Reflections of the Old European heritage in nowadays national cultures of southeastern Europe**

The many features in the national cultures of the Balkanic region and of Greece that find their origin in the heritage of Old Europe are a rich body in research on the impact of cultural memory among the peoples of southeastern Europe. Contours of a multifaceted identity, with which the people of today live and which they pass on to subsequent generations are revealed ever more (Haarmann 2019a: 250 f.):

– through their linguistic usage: with substrate elements of the Old European language (Poruciuc 1995: 35 ff., Haarmann 2003: 37 ff.);

– Through their orally transmitted stories and songs, with variants of the Great flood story and other prehistoric narrative motifs (Poruciuc 2010: 14 ff.);

– Through their folklore, with the hora or kolo dance, the ring dance from the Neolithic period, or ritual dances on the occasion of religious festivals (Ilieva and Shturbanova 1997);

– Through their craftsmanship, with the ancient building tradition of the *plinthos* wall, wattle walls plastered with mud on a stone foundation; with the use of clay stamps to apply decoration and traditional cultural symbols (Naumov 2008: 73 ff.);

– Through their familiarity with old building and construction forms with the design of ovens or with utensils and vessels that have not changed their shape for millennia (Bucur et al. 1986, Vasileva 2003: 50);

- Through the cut of folk costumes and their accessories as well as the accompanying hairstyles, with forms and motifs known from Old European decorated figurines (Bădocan 2007, Komitska et al. 2000);
- Through their cultural symbols: with logos of certain occupational groups alluding to the motifs of neolithic clay stamps and with traditional motifs woven into textiles (Waller 2010);
- Through customs and ritual acts at folk festivals and religious festivities, with the ritual baking of bread and the decoration of symbolic loaves of bread as votive offerings (Vasileva 2003: 9, 14 f., 41 f., 86, 115, 152);
- Through religion based on the virgin Mary, with its allusions to the cult of ancient goddesses, the daughters and granddaughters of the figure of the Neolithic goddess (Pelikan 1996);
- Through burial customs, with the two-stage practice of the Orthodox Christians of Greece, i.e. the primary burial of the corpse; the secondary burial of the bones of deceased persons after the decomposition process is complete (Danforth 1982);
- Through all kinds of ideas about the magical effect of things or symbols, with echoes of ancient numerology, belief in witches and spirits (Bilţiu 2007).

Such features are being extensively studied (e.g. Poruciuc 2010, Haarmann 2011, 2014, 2018). Old European cultural heritage includes material elements as well as symbolic forms i.e. the intellectual culture. The domain of intellectual culture is the very foundation of cultural memory, and detailed documentation has been compiled for this area in particular:

> "The outlines of what was to become classical mythology can be perceived in prehistoric items unearthed by archaeologists, but such outlines also appear to be (paradoxically, from a chronological standpoint) 'foretold' in folk productions recorded only as late as modern times. And just as certain features of prehistoric shrines eventually evolved into basic parts of Christian churches […], much of what we know as mythology derived, more or less directly, from the ritual-cultural life of prehistoric peasants." (Poruciuc 2010: xiv)

In recent years, the search for traces has made a decisive contribution to building up new knowledge about the Old European cultural heritage. Special attention is paid to the roots of Greek civilization since documentation for that domain reaches back to the third and second millennia BCE.

The new findings are also instrumental to support the cultural self-awareness of the people who currently live in the lands where the Danube civilization once flourished and who recognize that this Old European heritage is mirrored in their own history. The organic whole of contact situations involving the culture and language of the people in Old Europe and the lifeways of people of Indo-European affiliation is highly complex and requires the interplay of interdisciplinary research methods.

2. Foundations of Old European worldview and the imprint on cultural self-awareness

A testimony for the continuation of Old European via ancient Greece to modern times is borrowed terminology in various domains. There is a megasymbol of ancient worldview which came to infuse religious traditions, to shape spiritual conceptualizations, eventually to permeate philosophical discourse and to open new horizons for looking at life, and this is *psyche*.

The fundamental concepts of Old European worldview could not be lost since "[...] these most persistent features in human history were too deeply implanted in the psyche" (Gimbutas 1989: 318). The statement made by Gimbutas is crucial because it points at the heart of the problem of cultural continuity in the horizon of time. It is noteworthy that, for the key term *psyche* ("psyche" = "life; vitality; soul") in ancient Greek, no cognate parallels can be found in other Indo-European languages. In addition to being isolated among cognate languages the phonetic structure of this expression points to pre-Greek origin (Beekes 2010: 1671 f.). This means that the idea of *psyche* had been conceptualized by the indigenous population of Old Europe and that the Indo-European immigrants to the region adopted the idea together with the word for it from their predecessors.

Since the times when the expression *psyche* is first recorded in literary sources (i.e. eighth century BCE, in Homer's *Iliad*) it is used with a great diversity of meanings. In a modern observer's view, soul relates to human beings. Contrasting with such a modern restrictive definition was the common belief of people in antiquity that a soul resides in everything living which includes animals and plants. Therefore, the following shades of meaning of the key term *psyche* have to be perceived in their unrestricted expanse (see Liddell and Scott 1883, p. 2026 f.):

- "breath as the sign of life" (corresponding to Latin *anima*);
- "life, spirit, vitality";
- "aspiration";
- (metaphorically) of things "dear as life";
- "the departed soul, spirit, ghost, shade" (seen as winged creature);
- "the soul or spirit (of a person)";
- "the soul, heart";
- "mind, understanding";
- "appetite";
- "butterfly" (e.g. in Aristotle's *History of animals* 551a14, Plutarch *Moralia* 2.3.2);

- "cicada".

The association of the psyche with cicadas is imbued with spirituality, reflecting the inventiveness of people in antiquity to establish connections between the realm of animals and the cultural space of human beings.

> "Beyond their basic biological characteristics, cicadas were associated with a number of broader concepts and myths. Their incessant sound was typically characterized as a musical 'song,' and one that was 'sweet' or 'shrill'. This gave

the cicadas a connection to the Muses [as in Plato's *Phaedrus* 230c], poetry, and the rhetorical arts more generally. Other deities with whom the cicadas were associated include Athene, nymphs, and Pan, the last of these because noontime is the hour when he sleeps (and so is not to be disturbed by mortals). This connection between the cicada and divinity goes beyond just its song. The cicada itself was seen as godlike or divine, in virtue of the fact that it sheds its skin." (Werner 2012: 137)

In the focal signifier *psyche* is encapsulated in the code of the Old European concept of spirituality that has left its mark on the Greek mind (Haarmann 2013a: 164-167, 258-261). A concept which is closely related to describe phases of presence (or absence) of the soul is *coma* ("state of motionlessness of the body; state of the absence of the soul"), this too of pre-Greek coinage (Beekes 2010: 814).

Plato is the first philosopher to systematically discuss aspects of the soul in several of his dialogues. Central topics in his discourse are the quality of the soul to be immortal, to be tripartite and to be self-moving. According to the chronological order of their completion, the dialogues in which matters of the soul are treated form the following sequence: *Phaedo, Phaedrus, Republic, Timaeus, Laws* (Haarmann 2017: 127-146). Plato also is the first to elaborate on the concept of the World Soul (in his dialogue *Timaeus*, 34b – 37c).

A goddess of pre-Greek origin (i.e. Hecate) is personified as the source of the World Soul, its divine mother (Majercik 1989: 4). The association of Hecate with the World Soul is best known from the so-called Chaldean Oracles (fragmentary texts from the second century CE). The World Soul "springs from Hecate as "Source of Sources" (*pege pegon*, [...])" (Turner 2010: 221). "The theory of a soul of the world (*psyche tou kosmou, anima muni*) is almost as ancient as European philosophy itself" (Vassányi 2011: 1).

Given the manifold shades of meaning expressed by the term *psyche* one may conclude that we deal with a key concept of Old European worldview that was chosen, as a topic, by some pre-Socratic philosophers (e.g. by Heraclitus; Schofield 1991), later specified and rationalized by Plato and, through Plato's writings and later Platonism, found its way into the European philosophical tradition.

3. Communality and the issue of egalitarianism

When Marija Gimbutas talked about gender equality and peaceful social relations in Old Europe her assessment was ridiculed and stigmatized as "feel-good nostalgia" of a world order that, allegedly, never existed. And yet, as investigations into the web of interactions within individual settlements and among settlements made progress, the ingredients of community life under the auspices of economic and social egalitarianism became discernible. The priority of egalitarian ways of life can be reconstructed on the basis of certain leitmotifs which serve as indicators of social orientation in the communities of ancient Europeans.

Among these leitmotifs are burial customs and grave goods. There is consensus among archaeologists that grave goods are diagnostic markers which illustrate the degree of social differentiation in prehistoric society (Yakar 2011: 27 f.). If grave goods are distributed in a way which suggests that no distinctions existed between rich and poor or between men and women, the graves are interpreted as belonging to an egalitarian society without social differentiation or hierarchy. This was the case in Old Europe. The presence of a ruling élite in a society is reflected in the grave goods of members of the upper class. Here, we find a marked difference between graves of the rich and the poor, as it begun with the switch to Indo-European culture.

What was also alien to the Greeks because of their Indo-European origin was the custom to the indigenous, i.e. pre-Greek settlers not to distinguish between grave goods according to reputation.

Analyses of grave goods and of the layout of settlements across Old Europe suggest this to a society with egalitarian structures, with social and economic equality, with all members of the community sharing in the profits from the agrarian surplus and trade. With good reason these socio-economic conditions governed by collaboration among members in social groups have been described as the Old European oecumene (or commonwealth) based on egalitarian principles (Haarmann 2011b: 88 ff., 2019c). In the Danube civilization, egalitarianism manifested itself in two spheres, the economic and the social.

The layout of ancient settlements may also serve as a mirror of the social organization of a community. Distinctive complexes of richly furnished buildings (separated from ordinary small-size dwellings) point to the presence of a social élite. For the inhabitants of settlements whose layouts lack such distinction between ordinary and elaborate buildings, it can be rightly concluded that the social infrastructure was egalitarian.

The characteristic type of settlement in Old Europe is known by its original name, and this is *kome*. This expression is an element in the vocabulary of the language spoken in the regions of Old Europe, and it was adopted as a loanword by the ancestors of the Greeks who encountered the descendants of the ancient Europeans in the land that came to be called 'Hellas'. *Kome* ("village from old times") in ancient Greek points to a pre-Greek settlement which is open and not fortified by trenches, fences or palisades. This is reminiscent of the spirit of peaceful relationships between settlements in Old Europe where defensive fortifications were not needed. The administration in the *kome* settlements was organized in an egalitarian institution: a village council where men and women could be members. The trust of the inhabitants of a *kome* in their municipal council, that is in the elected representatives of this body, was evidently justified by their integrity, reliability, prudence and foresight, so that their decisions were approved by the majority of the community (LaBGC and Haarmann 2019).

The ancient Greeks showed themselves impressed by community life governed by self administration without a chief since that was totally alien to them and their system of hierarchy, maintained as something absolutely dominant and indispensable from their descendance from the Indo-Europeans pastoral society. Yet he idea of the *kome* village council was retained in the Greek settlements, the *demoi* (plural of *demos*) but women were excluded from being elected for the council.

- **Economic egalitarianism**

Economic egalitarianism is apparent in extended trade relations, where villages exchanged goods among themselves and with larger settlements. There is no evidence that any of the larger settlements dominated the economy of surrounding villages. In the context of economic egalitarianism, trade contacts evolved as relationships of mutual advantage, making the community a commonwealth. Among the preferred trade goods were obsidian, shells (spondylus, in particular), salt and copper. In addition, objects with ritual functions, such as figurines, were considered valuable goods for gift-giving and for a ritual to strengthen relationship.

A major indicator of economic egalitarianism is communal landownership, and this was common in the era of Old Europe. There is no evidence for private landownership in the Danube civilization while proof for the functioning of communal landownership is available. The idea of communal landownership is that the community (represented by a village council) distributes patches of land to local farmers. Once the farmers gain earnings from their crops they have to pay the rent for their land to the village council. This system developed even to the advanced stage of a leasing system, also including communal services of all kinds.

The principle of communal landownership did not vanish once communities in Old Europe came under the political control of Indo-European migrants from the steppe region. There are cases of a longterm continuity of the leasing system through the Bronze Age into the Mycenaean era and beyond. So to speak a showcase of longevity is the organization of landownership in the community of Thorikos (or Thoraces), a place known from antiquity, located in the coastal area of the Aegean in the historical landscape of Attica.

Thorikos was founded in the late fifth millennium BCE. The Greeks of antiquity were aware that this community was an original settlement of the ancient civilization, categorized as *kome*. In the region of Thorikos, rich deposits of silver and lead were discovered. The exploitation of those natural resources started around 3200 BCE, that is the beginnings date to the transition period between the Old European Copper Age and the Bronze Age (Laffineur 2010: 712 f.). In the second millennium BCE, during the Mycenaean era, Thorikos started to flourish and developed into a center of metal production in the landscape of Laureotika.

Since the times when the natural resources of Thorikos had been exploited the silver mines remained under communal ownership, that is they were never owned by private owners. The primacy of communal ownership is documented for the Mycenaean era in texts written in Linear B and it continued into Greek antiquity. The members of the community council gave licenses to mining experts from outside the community who were then authorized to extract silver. These had to pay a portion of their earnings to the community. The surplus was distributed equally among the inhabitants of Thorikos.

During the period of classical antiquity, Thoraces flourished to become one of the richest communities in the Athenian state (Bintliff 2012: 270). The community with its long history, dating to the times of Old Europe, developed into an urban center, and its status changed from a *kome* to that of a komopolis. In the scholarly literature one finds the term "village state" as a translation for komopolis (Kirsten 1956).

In the sixth century BCE, the community was rich enough to afford building a theater which is among the oldest in Greece. Thorikos ranged among the fourteen communities in Greece that had a theater. In the fourth century BCE, the space for spectators was enlarged to accommodate up to 3200 visitors (see a model of the theater of Thorikos in Roselli 2011: 69).

While from 6th to 4th century BCE in Athens, the assembly of the city council (*ekklesia*) met on the Pnyx hill in the vicinity of the Acropolis, in Thorikos, the members of the *kome* council gathered in the theater for their sessions. This place achieved a leading role as a central point for meetings of members of one of the Greek tribes (Akamantis). The historical development of the community ended abruptly when, in 86 BCE, the Romans destroyed Thorikos during their military campaigns to conquer all of Greece. The city was later rebuilt. During the turbulent times that followed the end of antiquity, Thorikos was deserted in the course of the sixth century CE.

Thorikos is a model case demonstrating longevity of priority of communal economic interests. It is apparent that the primacy of communal landownership that had originated in Old European times proved its usefulness as a foundation for community administration. So it was kept up throughout the various periods of local history. The fundamental idea of a leasing system, that is letting the rights for operations via rent to external professionals, was not abandoned after Thorikos had been deserted by its inhabitants in the early Middle Ages. Instead, the idea has experienced a revival in modern times. Cases of natural resources under communal administration functioning on the basis of leasing are known, on various scales, from Europe (i.e. Andalucia) and from Africa (i.e. Botswana); (LaBGC & Haarmann 2019; an English version appeared in 2021).

And also in Asia the economic egalitarianism described here for the communities in Old Europe was characteristic of the communities that flourished in the valleys of the Indus and Sarasvati rivers in India, in the third and second millennia BCE. Egalitarianism manifests itself in lively trade relations where villages exchanged goods among themselves and with towns. There is no evidence to show that the towns would have dominated the economy of the villages.

- **Social egalitarianism**

The principle of social egalitarianism is reflected in the absence of a marked distinction between the social roles of the sexes in community life, something which is typical of a society with a hierarchy. Equality between the sexes implies matrilinearity or matrifocality (with women as prominent figures in lineages); (see Bott 2009: 106 ff. for a critical analysis of the duality of matrilinearity and patrilinearity). The prominent status of women in Old European society has been characterized as "matristic" by Gimbutas (1991: 324 ff.). Prominence must not be confused with dominance. The prominent status of women points to the fact that women had a privileged role in kinship relations, in trade, household and in certain professions (e.g. pottery-making). This does not mean that women would have suppressed men or marginalized their functions as husbands and fathers. According to modern anthropological research, cases of a sociopolitical dominance of women in historic societies are rare exceptions (e.g. the Naxi in southern China); (see Haarmann 2007: 162 ff. for an outline).

There is an assessment about the roles of the sexes in Çatalhöyük, made by Ian Hodder who has been leading the excavations there since 1993. Hodder (2004) states that there was no distinction in the social status between the sexes. This statement would in fact relate to the oldest agrarian society about which we have some reliable data, reaching back into the seventh millennium BCE. Ironically, Hodder does not perceive the resemblance between his findings about social egalitarianism at Çatalhöyük and those made by Gimbutas for Old Europe. On the contrary, he criticizes Gimbutas for something she never said or intended: "Marija Gimbutas [...] argued forcefully for an early phase of matriarchal society, [...]" (Hodder 2006: 208). In fact, Gimbutas' reconstruction of society in Old Europe explicitly avoids a misunderstanding about female dominance:

> "The burial rites and settlement patterns reflect a matrilineal structure, whereas the distribution of wealth in graves speaks for an economic egalitarianism. [...] Indeed, we do not find in Old Europe, nor in all of the Old World, a system of autocratic rule by women with an equivalent suppression of men." (Gimbutas 1991: 324)

It is undoubtedly Gimbutas' merit to have highlighted a prominent example of an oecumene model of society for the Old World, thus providing a differential for the prototype axiom of Mesopotamian studies. This emphasis of women holding a prominent position in the prehistoric communities of southeastern Europe is not only typical of the works of Gimbutas, Eisler, Marler and others, but also of the same Hodder (1992: 67), though ignorant of Gimbutas' standpoint, who stresses "the central importance and power of women as reproducers and as the nodes of links to other lineages".

The gender equality of Old European did not continue into Greek antiquity since this leitmotif of egalitarian society was overformed by the patriarchal structures of Indo-European coinage, introduced by the ancestors of the Greeks. Yet, the ideal concept of community life with gender equality had a revival on a theoretical level, in the fourth century BCE, in the work of Plato.

Plato has been referred to as a "patriarchal" writer by some feminists (e.g. Barbara Freeman 1988) while others characterize his position in gender issues as "unambiguously feminist" (Gregory Vlastos 1994). How can such contradictions in evaluation be explained in light of the huge amount of literature that has been produced to highlight Plato's intellectual input?

As for the selective nature of some studies on Plato's gender issues, Stella Sandford's study *Plato and sex* (2010) may be mentioned. This author delimits her analysis of the topic 'sex' to some of Plato's works (i.e. *Republic, Symposium, Timaeus)* but leaves out other dialogues where gender issues are of equal importance (i.e. *Menexenus, Phaedrus, Laws*).

Plato's discourse on the role of women in society is based on an understanding of gender equality.

> "His provision would entail that a woman [...] is qualified not only to hold office herself after a process of lot-taking or election or both, but also to vote to elect others, both male and female. She would be entitled to act as a juror in any kind of case, both private and political, and to take a full part in the highest councils of the state, becoming a member of the *boule* (council), *ekklesia* (assembly), the Board of thirty-seven Guardians of the Laws (the chief executive officials) and presumably even the Nocturnal Council, the supreme governing body." (Saunders 1995: 593)

"In contrast, Aristotle's position [...] advocates a different status for women and men that is not negotiable" Mayhew 2004). Aristotle asserts: "As far as the sexes are concerned, man is by nature superior and woman inferior, man ruler and woman subject" (Politics, 1254b13-14). "From the chronological standpoint [...] it is noteworthy that the older

Plato, Aristotle's mentor, is more intellectually advanced than his student" (Smith 1983).

Given the Athenian reality that excluded women (and slaves) from any public social and political life, Plato's written work, as well as the founding of his Academy, which was open to both men and women, can be considered revolutionary. As a precaution, he had the academy established outside the limits of legal reach. As the owners of the land on which the Academy was functioning Plato names the Muses. This connection to mythical sacred beings made the philosopher „immune" vis-à-vis worldly legislation and, he thus managed to avoid possible punishment, up to and including the loss of civil rights.

Plato's reflections on the nature of divine law, apparently, the most crucial implication for the philosopher is that the contents of what the law stipulates is binding for all citizens in the imagined ideal state (*Laws*, book VII: 804d-e). Here, principles of communality and gender equality become transparent and echoes the cooperative nature of social relations in Old European communities, echoes transmitted to Plato via the teachings of Plato's mother, Periktione, herself a philosopher, who composed the treatise *On the harmony of women* (see Appendix II in Haarmann 2020).

> "If Plato were living today and he had access to our facts, which are far more favorable to the pertinent abilities of women, he would be even a greater supporter of the equality of women. His justice would blindfold gender everywhere that justice reaches." (Santas 2010: 117)

Plato's standpoint on the possibility of women holding office in the ideal state provided far-reaching perspectives for equality on the political level. Yet, it took more than 2,200 years, well into the twentieth century, for Plato's ideas about the participation of women in public affairs (communal and state offices) to materialize.

4. Focusing on a female divinity: The heiresses of the Great Goddess

Classical mythology is a cultural domain which we so readily address as 'Greek' despite its abundance of pre-Greek figures, motifs and narrative strategies. Something that is obvious for everybody who engages in the study of ancient Greek mythology and religion is the abundance of female divinities (Haarmann and Marler 2008: 48 f.). This impression holds true not only with respect to the classical era, that is from the fifth century BCE onward, but also for the remote past. The pantheon of the Mycenaean Greeks in the second millennium BCE was as peopled by female divinities.

> "The most noticeable characteristic of Mycenaean Greek religion is the preponderance of female deities. The most important of these is po-ti-ni-ja /Potnia/ as both the mother of the Earth and the protectress of animals. Her sanctuaries are to be found in different places and from their names she becomes known as A-ta-na-po-ti-ni-ja /Athanai Potniai/, Da-pu-ri-to-jo-po-ti-ni-ja /Laburinthoio Potnia/, [...]" (Ilievski 2000: 365)

The preponderance of goddesses in Greek mythology stands in stark contrast to the male-dominated pantheon of Proto-Indo-European coinage (Mallory and Adams 2006: 408 ff.). When the early Greeks absorbed the cultural heritage of the ancient Europeans they also adopted the cults of female deities. The magnitude of this process of adaptation to non-Indo-European cult life may be reflected in a pertinent deviation of Greek terminology from the nomenclature in most other branches of Indo-European. And this concerns the key term 'god'. It is noteworthy that

> "[…] at an early stage the Greeks seem to have dropped the term *deiwós*, 'god', attested in nearly all branches of the Indo-European family, which is a derivative of IE *dyew-/diw-*, which denoted the bright sky or the light of day. Instead they opted for *theós*, originally 'having the sacred', cognates of which have been recognized in Armenian and, rather recently, in Lycian, Lydian and Hieroglyphic Luwian. The change must have happened at an early stage of Greek history, as it had already taken place in Mycenaean times, the oldest period for which we have evidence regarding the gods of ancient Greece, […]" (Bremmer 2010: 1)

Indeed, the concept 'having the sacred' (*theos*, rendered as te-o in Linear B texts of the Mycenaean era) applies to the whole range of pre-Greek divinities – most of them chthonic (i.e. earthbound) – that were integrated into the Greek pantheon, but any association with the bright sky and the light of day as in Indo-European terminology does not reflect their true nature. Eventually, the all-embracing figure of the Old European Goddess transformed into many different divine personalities, distinguished according to their functions.

For the ancient Aegean cultures of the Bronze Age, the presence of a major female deity – presiding over a pantheon of gods – can be reconstructed. The pre-Indo-European heritage of the goddess cult is best known from ancient Crete with its Minoan civilization that flourished in the second millennium BCE. The opinions of scholars are divided over the fabric of Minoan religion. Some assume the presence of one mighty female divinity while others reconstruct a pantheon of gods and goddesses. Even if Minoan religion knew various divinities, the prominence of female deities among them remains striking. "That a powerful goddess of nature was the chief deity of the Minoans [...] has never been seriously questioned" (Marinatos 1993: 147).

The heritage of the „strong women" is reflected in the goddess cults of classical antiquity where the figure of the Old European Goddess has proliferated into a multitude of individualized divinities that continue – each in her own cult and with a religious and mythical network involving pre-Greek terminology – specific aspects and qualities of the former Great Goddess:

- Gaia – Earth Goddess (worshipped at Delphi and at other places);
- Hera – goddess of fertility, of matrimony and childbirth, patron of the sacred precinct of Olympia;
- Demeter – the patron of agriculture (the Grain Mother);
- Hestia – the guardian of the hearth and the household;
- Artemis – the patron of nature and of wildlife, later goddess of urban life;
- Themis – the goddess of customary law and righteousness;
- Dike – the goddess of justice;
- Eirene – the divine guardian of peace;
- Eunomia – the goddess of lawful government;

- Eurynome – the Pelasgian pre-Greek goddess
- Athena – the patron of technologies such as pottery (the potter's icon was Athena's owl), ship-building and weaving, the patron of justice, of the arts and science.

The evidence for pre-Greek origins of the cults of these goddesses are their pre-Greek names. This is true for Gaia, Artemis, Hera, Hestia, Themis, Eirene, and Athena. The names of Eunomia and Eurynome in fact Greek even though their origin is pre-Greek. The domains of the goddesses adopted by the Greeks ranged from the most private (i.e. Hestia) to the most public (i.e. the state cult of Athena). Their functions were specialized (i.e. Eunomia) as much as comprehensive (i.e. Artemis). Female divinities were the protagonists at places which were of great significance for the formation of a sense of Greek unity (i.e. the role of Olympia and Delphi as focal points for Hellenicity). This was true for Gaia and Hera.

The figure of Athena around which Bronze Age traditions crystallize illustrates the decisive phase of transition from the late Bronze Age to the Iron Age. Pre-Greek Athena does not stand alone since also the archaeology of other divinities of pre-Greek times (e.g. Hera) confirms the grand theme of continuity of artifact production and of mentifacts (cultural and religious concepts). Cultic continuity

> "[…] includes the megaron on the acropolis of Tiryns, supposedly reconstructed to house a cult of Hera which continued a palace-based religion, besides the cult of Athena on the Athenian Acropolis, which also takes up a palace cult. The same scenario is proposed for Athena at Mycenae. The assumption that citadel sanctuaries carried on palace-centred Mycenaean cult is ultimately based on

the presumed divinity of the Mycenaean king, grounded in two Homeric passages (Iliad 6. 546-51, Odyssey 7. 80-1)." (Antonaccio 1994: 88 f.)

The female figures, with their attributes and epithets, offer insights into continuity from Old Europe times. In addition and difference to the Old European heritage, the mythic narratives about the goddesses and their interaction with male gods reflect various phases of the fusion process with Indo-European patriarchal culture in the course of which the male protagonists of the Greek pantheon marked their range of power vis-à-vis their female counterparts. In a comparative view of attributes that were valued by the ancient Greeks in association with gods and goddesses, the astonishing relativity in the importance of individual motifs is revealed. Although physical strength is the stereotyping asset of male gods and heroes, this aspect is not the decisive agent for a successful career. Apparently, female wisdom and diplomatic skills provide the underpinnings of power struggle for many a mythic narrative.

> "In Hesiod's *Theogony*, physical strength is less of a *motivating* force in succession than is generational strife, in the sense that a female figure, either a wife or a mother, always interferes in the process of succession. Although the physical strength of Zeus is often mentioned in the *Theogony*, in fact it is Gaia who is the dominant figure in plotting the succession and who plays the decisive, i.e. motivating, role." (Yasumura 2011: 77)

The most prominent example of the competition among female and male divinities is perhaps the relationship of Zeus and Hera although there also is a "third" player in this relationship which is little known.

The union of Zeus and Hera in Greek myth can be interpreted in metaphorical terms as marking the shift from pre-Greek to Greek cultural dominance. When this interpretation is embedded in the archaeological record of early Greece then one finds that the pre-Greek goddess Hera competed with the "first wife" of Zeus who was an Indo-European goddess.

> "His wife is Hera, a pre-Greek goddess of fertility. Diwia – the Indo-European partner of Zeus – was still worshipped in Mycenaean times and had her own shrine in Pylos, but was obviously replaced by Hera who appears together with Zeus and receives offerings at Zeus' sanctuary." (Ilievski 2000: 365)

Hera won the competition, and this can be interpreted as the resilience with which the pre-Greek substrate culture infused the structures of Greek civilization. At Olympia, Hera is worshipped on equal terms with Zeus, and this did not change until the advent of Christianity.

The goddesses of Old European origin, worshipped in the countries around the Mediterranean, could not be extinguished when the Christian faith started to spread. The "pagan" cults were officially abandoned but, in popular religiosity, many of the properties of the ancient divinities continued among those who converted to Christianity. The worship of the goddesses was transferred to the worship of the Virgin Mary.

The same was true for the functions of the ancient goddesses. They had been venerated, as patrons of childbirth, motherhood, of the caring for children, and guardians of home and household, and of the family. These functions were so fundamental as to be transferred to Mary. In the cultural memory of those who had formerly worshipped the ancient goddesses their functions fused with the worship of the Virgin Mary. This is true for the Egyptian Isis (nursing her child Horus) who was popular also among the Romans, the Greek goddesses Hestia (guardian of the hearth) and Hera (patron of childbirth and matrimony) or Athena (goddess of wisdom, protectress of the city and guardian of justice).

Among those Greek divinities whose features were absorbed by Mary, Athena may be the most revered:

> "By the time the Parthenon of Athens was dedicated to Mary as Mother of God in the sixth century, she had taken on many of the images and honours of the ancient goddesses as well as moving into many of their temples." (Shearer 1996: 118)

In many cities, pre-Christian temples were dedicated to Mary where the worshippers of the old days honored the new "queen of heaven". In the names of some churches, the memory of the previous "owner" of the place is encapsulated. One of the major churches in Rom may serve as an example to illustrate this naming pattern. This is the Basilica di Santa Maria sopra Minerva ("Basilica of Saint Mary over [the temple] of Minerva") which was built directly on the foundations of a temple originally dedicated to Minerva, the Roman equivalent of Athena.

Meaning and function of the Goddess changed over the centuries, especially with the implemented competition with male divinities in the patriarchal system of ancient Greece introduced by their Indo-European predecessors. It ranges in earlier forms of polytheism and later, in the dominance of a male god in monotheistic religions. But the worldview associated with the great force, imagined as female, was neither completely degraded nor abandoned: as Mary or Mother Earth the Great Goddess of Old Europe continues to be summoned by people searching for help. The continuity of the great force of goddesses in the Greek pantheon together with male gods proves the fundamental quality of experience of the Old European civilization. In the figure of Mary, this spirit has been preserved into our time.

5. Old European goddesses as patrons of Indo-European heroes

When the communities of the ancient Europeans with their social interaction following the principle of egalitarianism were first faced by the intruding Indo-Europeans with their patriarchal hierarchy and then imposed with it, they were also confronted with the Indo-European caste of warriors. Both completely alien to the peaceful ancient Europeans. The functioning of the newly introduced warrior caste produced a mindset the essence of which coagulated in myths of heroes.

Taking into account that the intrinsic connection between myth and society reflects a society's system it becomes evident that "the myths of a people were not only to some extent ciphers of their (often archaic) social structures, but they also reinforced social behaviour and served as divine charters for political realities" (Mallory 1989: 130). For example, in the society and mythology among Indo-Aryan people, that is among those Indo-Europeans who moved into India and called themselves Aryans, the warrior class functions as a pivotal category in the system of tripartition. The *ksatriyas* ("warriors as protectors of the community") are a late – and at the same time vivid – reflection of the warrior bands among the Proto-Indo-European pastoralists in the Eurasian steppe.

> "Whatever the theories that have been propounded concerning a Proto-Indo-European social organization, the group or segment operating in what Georges Dumézil identified as the *fonction guerrière*, his Warrior or Second

Function, that is, the function dedicated to the forcible defence or armed expansion of any given society, is one that evidently appears early and occupies an important social and possibly a political role." (Miller 1997: 631)

May be in order to fire up the spirit for fight a cult of heroes was established, in modern research called „celebrity culture (Barron 2014). Only those warriors were declared heroes who enjoyed glorious victory. No wonder that they looked for patronage, for divine support in their strife for fame (see Haarmann and LaBGC 2021 for a survey).

Astonishingly, in the monuments of visualized cultural memory when Indo-Europeans were on the way to gain the upper hand in Old Europe, we recognise a shift in focus from the depiction of heroes in arms to motifs that are familiar from the Old European heritage: women without weapons. In the imagery of stone stelae in the regions where the warrior caste emerged, that is in the steppe zone of southern Russia and Ukraine, the major motif is the warrior in arms. Yet, the major motif of imagery in the areas of Old Europe – the female figure – stands in stark contrast to the theme of the male hero. A splendid example is the stela called *La Dame de Saint Sermin sur Rance* (ca. 3300 BCE; Barile 2019: 30). Old-established sculptors had adopted the idea of stelae, most likely created after having heard by the traders to the noth of the stone stelae depicting men, but modified its major appearance to accommodate the spirit of the goddess of Old Europe, thus producing a female figure instead of a male one. Eventually, this new "hybrid" theme of the stela developed into a genre of figurative art in its own category, and it spread via the different trading routes to the south and to the west.

Whether deity or venerated female shaman, the stelae as memorial may have expressed the mindset of people, in a zeitgeist when women were assigned authority in community life, where the allegory of the primordial life-force expressed by the vegetation cycle was central to religious beliefs. This life-giving force is the reality that is advocated as the figure of the Great Goddess by Marija Gimbutas in her germinal works (Gimbutas 1974, 1989, 1991).

From the canon of Indo-European studies, the investigation of such stelae is excluded since the dominating female figure and major symbols (i.e., the spiral) cannot be reconciled with the tradition of Indo-European culture. "Many of the west Mediterranean stelae play little or no role in discussions of the early Indo-Europeans as they are assumed to depict female deities which cannot be convincingly accommodated by our evidence for Indo-European religion." (Mallory 1997: 544)

The prominence of goddesses in Old European art stands for the difference from the Indo-European system and marks its characteristic for the spiritual orientation before the arrival of the Indo-Europeans. The Indo-Europeans could not totally delete the basic ideas of this expression of spirituality when they began to settle in the core area of Old Europe and continued to infiltrate more and more regions of prehistoric Europe, but fused with their own-cultural traditions.

The members of the warrior caste, sensing the potential of divine protection, obviously began to place themselves under the protective patronage of goddesses. Because there is one thing that heroes fear the most: experiencing death in the absence of glory. These strong, yet fragile men, albeit ready to die, are not prepared to die without having achieved their ultimate goal: fame and glory. So they summon higher instances, the benevolent forces that may grant the warrior a heroic fate.

At first sight the interaction of a male hero with an ancient goddess may seem strange. It would be too simplistic to suspect some sort of chauvinism here, or imagine the heroes making the goddesses their accomplices. An approach from another angle is much more convincing. The heroes – caught in their own psychological straightjacket of being in need to become celebrated – intuitively feel that all their quests would be futile without the life-supporting force that only a female divinity can provide.

When the ancestors of the Greeks had arrived in the region of Attica they had certainly been puzzled by the presence of a mighty goddess whose abode was the Acropolis in the already existing town of Athens. This goddess with her pre-Greek name, Athena, was venerated by the descendants of the ancient Danubians and had prevailed through times of turmoil and unrest (Deacy 2001, 2008). The newcomers to Attica sensed that it would be futile to try to marginalize this powerful divinity and they tried to find a way to accommodate her and adopt her cult.

So they created a somehow adventurous myth about her birth. According to the mythical tradition, told in early literature (Homer, *Iliad*, book V, Hesiod, *Theogony*), Zeus married Metis, „wisest among gods and mortal men" (Hesiod, *Theogony* 885-900). Zeus received disturbing news from an oracle, revealing to him that he may have a son who would displace him as the mightiest of gods. In his fear, Zeus panicked and devoured Metis. Yet, the goddess had already conceived. After a while, Zeus suffered from a terrible headache and, one day, a child sprang off his head; and this was Athena, in full armor. Perhaps this "smoke-screen" hiding her origins and, at the same time, enhancing her ties to the Indo-European patrilinear tradition (from her father's side) made it easier for Greek men to acknowledge Athena's overall high status as a divinity and accept her as patron for the warrior caste.

Thus the idea of the hero seeking the protection and blessing of a female divinity made its way into Greek mythology, where goddesses are associated with heroes. A popular scene in Greek art depicting this relation is the suckling of the hero Herakles by the goddess Hera (figure 2).

Figure 2:   Hera suckling Herakles

(red-figure vase, c. 370 BCE; Oakley 2013: 64)

Among the accounts of interactions, either direct or indirect, between goddesses and heroes is Homer's *Iliad*, the collection of epic stories about the Trojan War. It begins with Homer summoning the goddess:

> "The rage of Achilles – sing it now, goddess, sing *through* me
>
> the deadly rage that caused the Achaeans such grief
>
> and hurled down to Hades the souls of so many fighters, […]." (*Iliad*, book 1.1-3)

The protective aspect of divine patronage is highlighted in various ways, and also in a very direct way when the goddess deflects a deadly arrow to save the hero's life (*Iliad*, book 4.118-21):

> "But then, Menelaus, the blessed gods did not forget you.
> Athena stepped out before you and with her hand
> deflected the deadly arrow, brushing it off
> as a mother brushes a fly from her sleeping child."

The pre-Greek Athena became supergoddess and the patron of many heroes. She supervises the construction of the ship for Iason, the Argo, and provides it with a "speaking beam". Under the leadership of Iason, the Argo and its crew, the Argonautai, set out on the voyage to the land of Aietes in search of the Golden Fleece, as told in the *Argonautika* by Herodoros in the fifth century BCE. Athena is also known to have given advice to Odysseus how to build a ship (*Odyssey*, book 5.234 ff.).

So divine patronage of heroes was assigned to female (not male) divinities and in this function goddesses were given a firm place in the cultural memory of people in Greek antiquity. The names of these goddesses – especially Hera and Athena – date to the era of Old Europe. And like their names also their cults have pre-Greek origins (Haarmann 2014: 25 ff.). The patronage of Old European female divinities for Indo-European heroes provides the ground for an amalgam of elements from both worlds in the fusion of different cultural contexts. Here they keep their role in the psyche as the universal and archetypical power. The cults of Hera and Athena are shining brightly in the afterglow of the cultural legacy of the Danube civilization.

A focal point for the glorification of Athena was the Acropolis in Athens, and the Parthenon Temple is undoubtedly the most famous sacral monument ever built to honour her. Parthenon means "temple of the virgin goddess". In the mythological tradition, Athena is a virgin (*parthenos*) and she never marries. This quality of being a virgin is also attributed to another of the pre-Greek goddesses who was adopted by the ancestors of the Greeks into their pantheon, and this is Artemis.

An earlier sanctuary dedicated to Athena is located in the north of the Acropolis (Hurwit 2000). This sanctuary housed the wooden statue of Athena, carved from olive wood, that was brought to Piraeus on the coast every year, in a ritual, and bathed in the sea. And on the site where the Parthenon was built archaeologists found remnants of a small shrine, suggesting that the place had already been considered sacred before the classical era – another evidence for the continuity of the veneration of Old European goddesses.

Concerning the adoption of Athena as patron for the warrior caste, introduced with the change from equality to patriarchal hierarchy, it is worth to take a brief look at the frieze of the Parthenon (see Haarmann & LaBGC 2021: 123 ff. for details).

In the metopes of the east frieze the conflict between the Gods and the Giants is illustrated. In these scenes, we see a sublime concerted action of the famous hero and the patron divinity. "Athena and Herakles fought side by side in battle, valiant warriors who made an excellent team. Athena so distinguished herself that she became known as Gigantoleteira or Gigantoletis ("She who destroyed the Giants")." (Connelly 2014: 64 f.)

The figure of the goddess Athena appealed to women and men alike:

— Athena was the patron of many a handicraft: as the patron of the craft of weaving she was in the hearts and minds of women; she was the favorite divinity summoned by potters, shipbuilders and architects;

— as the patron of democratic institutions Athena was venerated by law-makers, judges and politicians;

— as the patron of intellectual achievements she was praised by poets and philosophers;

— in her role as the patron of the arts she drew the special attention of artists to her cult;

— and the armed Athena (with spear and shield), the protectress of the city of Athens and guarantor of safety for everyone in the Athenian community, was revered by members of both sexes.

There is the special case of a prominent figure, Plato, who truly worshiped Athena in her manifold roles. Among all the goddesses, Plato, in his dialogue *Cratylus* (407b), praises the goddess in her elevated status as the guarantor of world order, "as mind (*nous*) and [divine] intellect (*dianoia*)". There could be no higher status than this, attributed to Athena in philosophical reasoning about the world (Haarmann 2019b: 79 f.).

In the Parthenon temple we can recognize the extension of the cult of the individual hero into the realm of collective self-glorification, of heroic Hellenicity. It is in the Parthenon with its most impressive monumental statue of Athena that the intimacy between fame-seeking heroes (of Indo-European coinage) and their divine protective patronage, personified in the figure of Athena (with her genealogy from the era of Old Europe), found its sublime expression.

6. The spirit of Olympia: The resurrection of an Old European institution

It is easy to illustrate the continuity of culture in the region of Olympia (in the northwestern part of the Peloponnese) because, according to the archaeological record, the area was continuously inhabited since the fifth millennium BCE. This makes Olympia a place that was frequented (and settled) by the ancient Europeans, and because of its high age Olympia formed part of the sociocultural network of the Old European civilization. The history of Olympia unfolded uninterruptedly during successive periods before the arrival of the Greeks there.

Among the relics pointing to a former presence of the ancient Europeans and their descendants are the foundations of some houses, an abundance of ceramic ware of different types and some figurines. Continuity of cultural activities in the area is documented for a prolonged period, from the Copper Age into the Bronze Age and beyond (Bintliff 2011: 243).

What is of special interest are the traces of the transitional phase when the site passed on from the indigenous inhabitants to the Greeks. The oldest constructions of Olympia, within the precinct of the Altis (sanctuary to the gods), are the temples of Hera, the wife of Zeus, and of Rhea, the mother of Zeus. When interpreting the chronology that is encapsulated in the mythical tradition a prolonged continuity of female goddesses and their cults is revealed that predates the introduction of a male god (i.e. Zeus) and its cult to the area.

Olympia is a truly mysterious place. The Olympic Games of ancient Greece, under the patronage of a male god, are known world-wide, but the much older tradition of festivals, associated with Hera, are not even known to all the visitors of Olympia, not to speak of a broader public. What is common to both traditions, the older female-dominated and the younger male-dominated, is that sportive competitions were organized there at intervals.

According to a widely-held view, the Olympics of antiquity were held for and by men only, with no women allowed to either participate or watch. This is a distortion of reality. Men as well as women participated in sportive games, only, the events of their festivals were segregated according to sex.

The early patron of festivities at Olympia was Hera, the pre-Greek Earth Mother, goddess of fertility and of the family. Although Hera's role in the Greek pantheon of classical times may seem somewhat marginal, this impression is misleading; "[…] the *Iliad* nevertheless preserves traces which suggest that Hera had once been a truly powerful goddess, and of course her importance in cult continued to be very significant in later times" (Yasumura 2011: 57).

At Olympia, rituals in Hera's honor were celebrated by young women, and women were the only ones allowed to take part in the sportive competitions, called Heraia. In Greek art, we find pictures of women-runners who compete with one another in the Heraia (figure 3).

Figure 3: A female runner at the Heraia of Olympia

(bronze figurine, c. 500 BCE; courtesy of The British Museum)

Once a year, the Heraia were held at the end of summer, comparable in their function to what we know as Thanksgiving. The women in the region of Olympia who gathered for the Heraia celebrated the blessing of the crops and they expressed their wishes for fertility, for themselves and for the domestic animals.

> "The girl-athletes, all maidens, run three foot-races according to age groups, always of the same length, one stadion minus a sixth (probably because a stadion is 600 ft, and a woman's pace is smaller than a man's). The girls do not compete naked – they wear a short dress – but their female power is nonetheless displayed and transmitted in what is, without question, an ancient fertility ritual, and perhaps, in part at least, a prenuptial rite of passage. As they run, their long hair flies loose, their dresses are unhitched at the right shoulder to expose a single breast, and their bare feet pound the track in direct contact with Mother Earth. The energy of their young bodies symbolises the dynamism of life." (Faulkner 2012: 85)

If it is true that sportive contests were held at Olympia in pre-Greek times then one would look for an expression from the substrate language to describe the essence of competition. Indeed, there is a key term of pre-Greek origin in ancient Greek, and this is *amilla* "a contest for superiority; a trial for strength" (Beekes 2010: 88). This word is also used in metaphorical meanings, for example, for a contest of marriage or a striving for wealth. The idea of *amilla* for expressing peaceful competition is quite different from what is described as *eris* "rivalry; conflict; military campaign". *Eris* was personified as the sister and companion of Ares, the god of war. *Eris* was known as the goddess who excites war. What was organized at Olympia was *amilla*, explicitly to avoid *eris*.

If Hera symbolizes the pre-Greek heritage of the region, then Zeus stands for the Greek presence. His temple is some

150 years younger than the temple of Hera, and it was completed in 456 BCE. The ancient Europeans who had settled at Olympia accommodated themselves and came to terms with the Greeks who took over the site, just like Hera accommodated herself to the master of all gods by becoming his wife. The union of Zeus and Hera in Greek myth can be interpreted in metaphorical terms as marking the shift from egalitarian pre-Greek to hierarchical, patriarchal Greek cultural dominance.

The men copied the idea of the sportive competitions from the women who venerated Hera and organized events every fourth year, honoring Zeus. According to common belief – already established in antiquity by the Greeks themselves – the first Olympic Games were held in 776 BCE. Altogether 293 games took place during antiquity, until 393 CE when the sporting event was abolished by the Roman emperor Theodosius I for its pagan association.

Myth has it that the Olympic Games were introduced by Heracles to honor Zeus. Heracles is also credited for having designed the Olympic Stadium although it is most probable that the site had been used by the female participants in the Heraia already earlier. The men who participated had to be Greeks, either as free citizens of the Athenian democratic state or as subjects in the various local kingdoms under Greek rulers. This means that the ancient Olympics were no international events in the modern sense but were restricted to Hellas, the Greek world. The victors of the Olympic contests adorned with twigs cut from a sacred olive tree that stood on the western side of the temple of Zeus, gained fame among the whole Greek population, in their home towns in particular.

In connection with the privileges granted to those who were victorious one can notice further similarities between the Heraia and the Olympics, with certain customs copied by the younger organization from the older.

> "Like male athletes at Zeus' s games, the female champions of the Heraia are also awarded olive wreaths, enjoy a sacrificial feast of beef, and have the right to erect victory monuments. No less telling of the hidden origins of the men' s games is the fact that the gold-and-ivory table for the olive wreaths is stored in the Temple of Hera, not that of Zeus: it is the goddess, not the god, who crowns the victors." (Faulkner 2012: 86)

Both the Heraia and the Olympics had a decisive effect for engendering a pan-Hellenic spirit of cohesion and a sense of cultural sameness.

> "It is often maintained that the terms 'Hellas' and 'Hellenes' were diffused throughout Greece via the sanctuary of Delphi. […] The construction of an ethnic community of Hellenes probably had more to do with Olympia than with Delphi, though the geographical conception of Hellas was indeed articulated through Delphi […]" (Hall 2002: 134 f.)

Like on the occasion of the Panathenaia in Athens, also at Olympia, the awareness of collective Greek identity (Hellenicity) was celebrated by the performance of a symbolic weaving-together of local interests that interlace in the collective fabric of Greek self-awareness. Like at Athens, also at Olympia, maidens wove a garment (*peplos*) to decorate the statue of the goddess. In Athens, this was the statue of Athena Polias and, at Olympia, the statue of Hera.

Symbolically, sixteen women were chosen to weave the sacred garment, each representing one of the sixteen communities of which the state of Elis was comprised.

> "Once in conflict, the sixteen "little cities" or "villages" – which Pausanias calls *poleis* – now find themselves reunited into a small federation thanks to the intervention of feminine wisdom. [...] Once its manufacture is completed, the new fabric is carried from the House of the Sixteen Women in Elis to the temple of Hera at Olympia, in order to replace the goddess's old cloak. This conveyance must have been spectacular, as it displayed to all of Elis the work of the Sixteen Women, into which the peace of the entire country was woven or rewoven. [...] It is to interweave what is different, contrary or hostile, in order to produce a unified, harmonious textile, worthy of covering the great goddess of Olympia herself." (Scheid and Svenbro 1996: 12)

The idea of the Olympics as a pan-Hellenic event vanished from public life for long, after the institution had been abandoned, and one could have imagined that it would have never reemerged again. But the idea of the Olympic Games never died. The tradition experienced a miraculous revival. Several attempts to revive it were made since the seventeenth century, but it took until the end of the nineteenth century before the breakthrough to achieve acknowledgment on an international scale was successful.

The first Olympic games of the modern age were organized in Athens in 1896. The competitions were restricted to men only. However, since the second games (in Paris in 1900), both men and women participated in the sportive competitions. The events preceding and surrounding the organization of the early games of the Modern Age are another fascinating story (Haarmann 2014: 143 ff.).

7. The Neolithic spirit in art and its timeless aesthetic appeal

The measure of an ancient civilization reaches far beyond the technological domains including religious patterns and worldview, values of social conduct, trends and fashions. If one wants to specify what makes a civilization then expressions in arts are good markers. In a society predominantly preoccupied with the struggle for survival artistic creations are rare for even a creative mind brimming with ideas will hardly find means and interest for art. In contrast, a prosperous society with social cohesion and open to the innovative spirit of creativity an artist has freedom for expressing thoughts and plenty of room to roam.

The advanced civilization of Old Europe was such a society, open for innovations, inventions, visions. This can be read from the many groundbreaking discoveries and the abundance and diversity of art objects found in the excavation sites. The stone stele depicting a female figure, most certainly influenced by the at that time still foreign culture of Indo-European art, shows inspiration instead of imitation.

Among the art objects admired by the public in the exhibition *The lost world of Old Europe – The Danube valley, 5000-3500 BCE* was a brought range of female figurines, beautiful examples of their spiritual importance within the cultural context of the societies that developed in southeastern Europe and eventually became the first advanced civilization of mankind.

The figurines seem to appeal to all human senses, ranging from their visible corporeality to the most sophisticated metaphorical meaning that might be evoked in the perceptive mind (Haarmann 2009: 85-132). They had sprung from the yearning to grasp an understanding of the great external strength that was felt and experienced behind the eternal cycle of life. The cyclic was reflecting the processes of nature. Natural catastrophes were reflecting death. The seasons made it possible to experience that all life returns and flourishes anew. As personified forces deities served to explain the inexplicable. Rituals and cults were associated to the hope to positively exercise influence for the well-being of individual and community (LaBGC & Haarmann 2021: 131-137). Thus the figurines filled the gap between yearing to understand and the impossibility to understand what is beyond us.

The history of making of these small-scale sculptures goes back in time to the Palaeolithic Age. The oldest artefacts date to some 34,000 years BP (before present; Conard et al. 2009: 244-271). And the making increased when the advanced civilization of Old Europe developed into a hub for the exchange of goods, knowledge and ideas. As sought-after items in exchange for other goods figurines were distributed by tradespeople – mostly women – to all directions, first over broadening contacts via the waterways of the Danube river and its tributaries and later also via the sea. Thus, they soon served as models for artists even in far away regions right across Europe and around the Mediterranean, and subsequently also reached other continents.

The connectedness of the Old Europeans far beyond the immediacy of the village or the urban neighbourhood, as well as their mindset is mirrored by the custom of giving figurines to exchange partners. Not as purposeful generosity, to score with a gift, but to make connectedness tangible. Figurines from clay were ritually broken, and the fragments kept by the partners. It was like a contract between them and the great strength symbolized by the figurine.

Thanks to Marija Gimbutas and many other scholars investigating in situ and reinvestigating with new methods the long-standing tradition of figurine-making is well-documented and its persistence throughout the Neolithic and Copper Ages is phenomenal.

Around 3000 BCE, a disrupture of figurine-making can be observed in the archaeological record and, seemingly, no more figurines were produced in the northern region. The explanation is Kurgan III, the third and most violent wave of Indo-Europeans forting their hierarchal, patriarchal system onto the indigenous population (see chapter 13) Large groups of Old Europeans migrated to the south where they continued with their traditions. With them the figurine-making shifted to the south where it continued even during the Helladic period (third millennium BCE) on the mainland as well as in the ancient Aegean cultures (i.e. in the Cyclades and in Minoan Crete) and also the Greeks in Hellas had taken up figurine-making.

Figurines

> "[…] were regularly produced throughout the Bronze Age in the Aegean, continuing an extant tradition from the Neolithic period […]. While Cycladic and Minoan products develop continuously, the mainland tradition of female figurines with exaggerated body features dies out in the Early Bronze Age […] The quantity of figurines present in

the archaeological record is indicative of their use. Fewer than 2,000 EC [Early Cycladic] figurines are known, produced over some 600-700 years in the third millennium BC. In contrast, at least 4,500 have been uncovered at a single site, Mycenae, dating between 1400-1100 BC." (Tzonou-Herbst 2010: 211)

No other ancient civilization produced a comparable abundance of figurines over such a long period of time, made from clay (glazed and unglazed), stone (mostly marble), metal (mostly gold) and after 3000 BCE increasingly from wax as well. The latter we know because the terminology of the production of wax figures has been preserved in the vocabulary of ancient Greek through loanwords from the Old European substrate language. It demonstrates the long-standing tradition of figurine-making, dating from Old Europe and persisting through the Bronze Age and ancient Greece.

Figurative art in Old Europe show a great diversity of forms, above all stylized small-scale sculptures, and all these forms are governed by the principle of a refined sense of abstractness (figure 4).

Figure 4: Sculptures from the regional Neolithic culture of Hamangia (Cernavoda, Romania; ca. 4800 BCE); (Kruta 1993: 84, 85)

a) Female figurine ("The Seated Woman")

b) Male figurine ("The Thinker")

The fascination of the works created by Old European artists, their descendants and those inspired by them lies in the reduction to the most expressive elements. It is only in the fifth century BCE, that Greek artists obviously felt determined to follow the doctrine established by Polykleitos in his book *Kanon*. It established the conventions of art styles, the 'canon', to be followed by many generations to come. This exclusive doctrine of western aesthetics remained valid beyond antiquity and well into the nineteenth century. These norms shaped "our own Greek training" (Gombrich 1960: 123) in art. Seemingly, the tradition of Neolithic art vanished into oblivion.

And yet, a sensational reflection of the Old European spirit in art occurred in the late nineteenth century with the work of Constantin Brancusi (1876 – 1957).

> "Brancusi played a pivotal role in developing the shifting and expanded identities that sculpture assumed in the twentieth century by shaping a body of work so imaginative, so multifarious, and so deeply felt that it has consistently drawn a sizeable audience, particularly from those most critical and attentive of all viewers of sculpture: other sculptors." (Chave 1993: 1)

It is clear from Brancusi´s biography that the main source of inspiration, during his early years, came from the prehistoric imagery of his home country Romania, what was known of it at the beginning of the twentieth century. Brancusi grew up in Oltenia, a region where the Old European heritage from the Neolithic and the continuation into the Bronze Age and beyond was best preserved. A distant reflection of that heritage was manifested in the traditional culture that continued into Brancusi's days (Miller 2010).

"The Thinker of Hamangia and his female counterpart and other recent excavations of the Neolithic Age in Romania offer us an unexpected providential confirmation of the high degree of authentic inspiration that led Brancusi to carve Ancient Figure at the beginning of 1907 and Wisdom of the Earth in 1907. Timeless contemporaneity mysteriously links Brancusi's work to the same source of inspiration as that of the Rumanian Neolithic Age thousands of years ago." (Varia 1986: 59 f.)

The Neolithic spirit is unmistakably present in his sculpture "Wisdom of the Earth" (1907) which reflects a unique distillation of Brancusi's early experiences with ancient imagery and it is a manifestation of how he perceived prehistoric society, earth-bound and with matrilinear structures (Varia 1986: 61).

Brancusi's emphasis on the Earth as the giver of life in the mindset of the early agrarian settlers in the region was conclusive and reasonably motivated. In as much as "The Thinker" could be categorized as one of the works of modern art, "Wisdom of the Earth" could range among the pieces of Neolithic art. In his own words, Brancusi intended to create a female figure "beyond personality", a character imbued with the mystery of a prototype of cosmic dimensions. In this again, the modern artist intuitively sensed the spirit of Neolithic imagery whose many forms bear witness to Brancusi´s timeless endeavor (Kruta 1993).

The impression of Brancusi's Neolithic inspirations reached further after 1904, once he had moved to France. The major museums for prehistoric art in Paris, the Musée du Louvre and the ethnographical collection of the Musée de l'Homme, offered insights into Neolithic imagery other than from

Romania, Cycladic idols for one and inspired Brancusi's art of his early years in France. "Today, […], it is easy for us to observe that a work by Brancusi resembles a Cycladic sculpture. But we may just as easily feel that a Cycladic work looks like a Brancusi" (Renfrew 1991: 174).

The revitalization of the Old European art in the works of Constantin Brancusi is the achievement of one single individual, without the cooperative efforts of a group of activists. Brancusi's exceptional work was the beginning of the movement of modern art.

In 2019, the Romanian filmmaker Viorel Costea completed a documentary film about Brancusi, highlighting the essence of the revival of the Old European spirit. Viorel Costea and his crew filmed at various locations in Romania (Hobita, Târgu Jiu, Craiova, Bukarest), in Paris (Brancusi's workshop at the Centre Pompidou) and in New York (Museum of Modern Art).

8. The Danube script (c. 5500 – c. 2600 BCE):
Sign inventory, social functions and derivations

The Old European societies shared a system of written signs called Danube script or Balkan scripts. It contains a broad variety of letters and a punctuation for numbers. This Neolithic communication system of signs and symbols has a striking resemblances with motifs of earlier times, in particular with the signs that one finds in the Mesolithic age in the cultural layer of Lepenski Vir and the rich symbolism of its imagery (Boric 1999), the immediate predecessor of the Vinča tradition (see Brukner 2002 for an outline). Most illustrative is the assemblage of signs on a spherical stone (figure 5). Such abstract motifs repeat themselves, with a delay of several hundred years, in the inventory of Vinča signs.

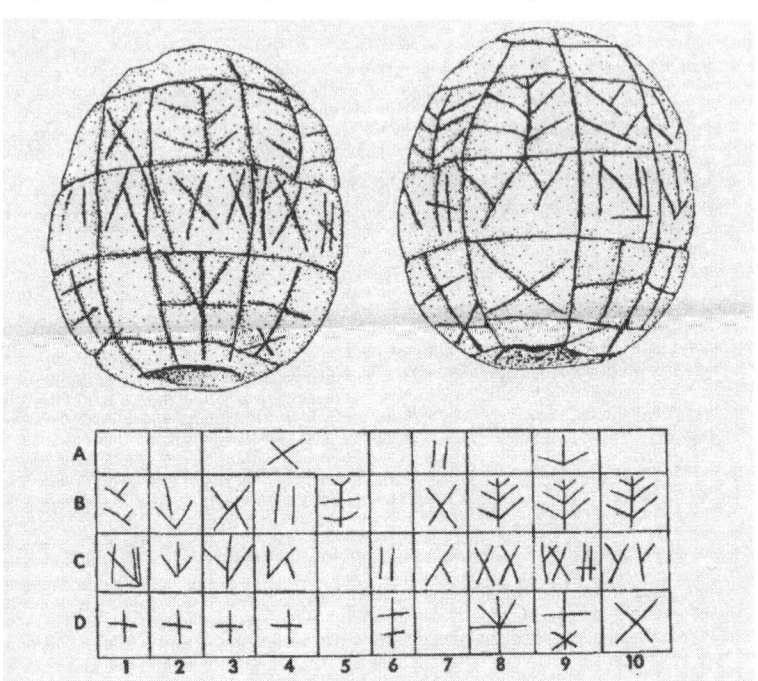

Figure 5: Signs on a spherical stone from Lepenski Vir

(Winn 1981: 259)

It has been suggested that the symbolism of the hunter-gatherers who frequented Lepenski Vir and other Mesolithic sites such as Vlasac and Padina in the seventh millennium BCE should be identified as "'signs of all time' [...] which might have been associated with religious beliefs and practices, altered states of consciousness and shamanic rituals" (Budja 2005: 65).

The oldest Neolithic variety of written signs and symbols in southeastern Europe (Maxim et al. 2009) is known from objects found in Transsylvania (Turdaș and Tărtăria). They draw on visual motifs in the iconography of earlier periods, i.e. Lepenski Vir and from cave paintings and rock carvings of the Balkan region. Basic motifs of this earlier iconography reflect community life by those hunter-gatherers who went through a process of acculturation, adopting farming and an agrarian way of living.

As a master/mistress of ceremonies the shaman retained his/her prominent role for the sustainability of the living-conditions in the early agrarian communities, and the shaman was in control of writing as a potent means of communication with the spirit-world. The transfer of iconographic symbols from pre-agrarian to agrarian media can be illustrated, among others, for the basic motif of the spiral that features, in the Danube script:

> "Paradigmatic was the act of attaching spirals – an old symbol on the new media – ceramic vessels – that had been incorporated into existing hunter-gatherers' ritual practices and symbolic structures (Lepenski Vir). This principle was evidently maintained in farmers' contexts, as identical pots have been embedded in similar symbolic structures or associated with prestigious artefact sets in trapezoidal pit-dwellings, […]" (Budja 2005: 65).

It seems reasonable to conclude that the drive toward the specialization of sign use in southeastern Europe, from the context of hunter-gatherers' iconography to written communication in the early agrarian communities originated on the continuum of ritual practices under shamanic supervision (Budja 2004). When assessing the experiments with writing technology in the European Neolithic from this viewpoint it becomes conceivable why and how basic shamanistic motifs came to form the core of the inventory of the Danube script (Haarmann 1995).

With the rise and spread of agrarian lifestyles in the Balkan region the repertory of cultural symbols and signs also proliferates. During the sixth millennium BC, when the use of abstract symbols and signs in the Danube region began a period of rapid expansion, this was not the sudden leap of the human mind into a hitherto unknown dimension. Rather, this phenomenon is indicative of the intensification of a process of experimenting with symbol-making that had been developing over millennia.

In southeastern Europe, the use of signs reached a higher organizational level than elsewhere, eventually developing into systematic forms of notation and an archaic form of writing (see Haarmann 2008 for an analysis of the Danube script and its organizational principles). The vivid and widespread use of writing technology and other forms of visual communication (i.e. cultural symbolism) favoured by the growing network of trade relations via the Danube river and its tributaries as the most frequented routes became typical for Old Europe (map 2).

Map 2: Sites with finds of inscriptions in the cultural provinces of the Danube civilization

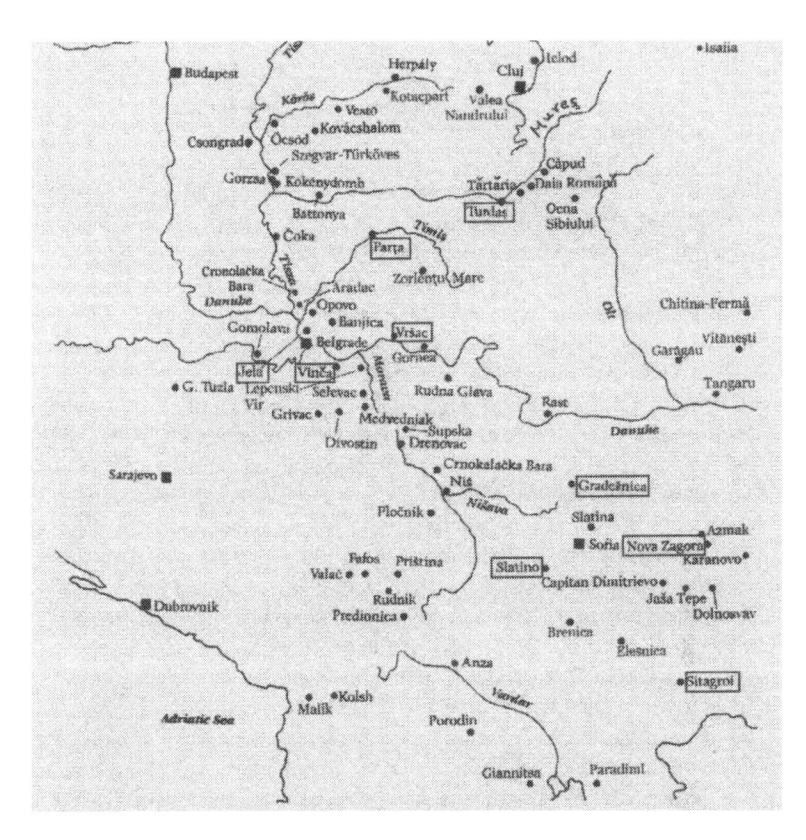

(irradiation centers for the use of writing are bordered; Merlini 2004, fig. II, with additions)

The richness of signs and symbols in southeastern Europe shows considerable variation in space and time (Haarmann 2010). Core symbols such as the spiral, the meander, the V sign and others are wide-spread while other symbols have a more limited range and are restricted to certain regions (figure 6).

Figure 6: Sign inventory of the Danube script (selection)

a) Iconic signs

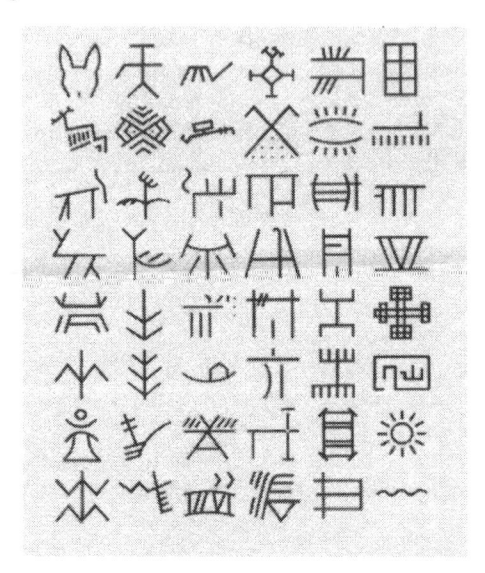

b) Abstract signs

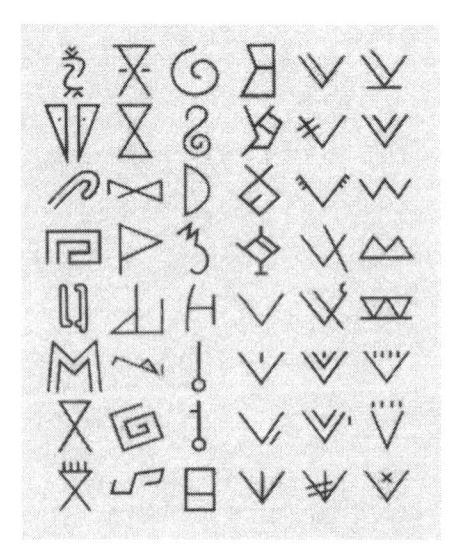

(Haarmann 1995, fig. 32)

The use of writing technology in the societies of Old Europe spread widely. Inscribed objects have been found at more than 180 sites (in 13 states) throughout southeastern Europe, concentrating mainly on the territories of Serbia, Romania and Bulgaria (see Merlini 2009a: 751 ff. and Haarmann 2010: 155 for surveys).

This tradition of writing eventually declined, surviving until c. 2600 BCE in western Ukraine but was revived in the ancient civilizations of the Aegean (Crete, the Cyclades) after an hiatus of several hundred years through descendants of Old Europe. The oldest documentation of written texts is in the Minoan script Linear A, which itself became the source of inspiration for other writing systems: Linear B for writing Mycenaean Greek, scripts of ancient Cyprus (Cypro-Minoan, Cypriote-Syllabic), scripts in the Near East such as Levanto-Minoan in Syria and Philisto-Minoan in Palestine (Haarmann 1995, fig. 195). The Aegean tradition of linear writing partly inspired the composition of the sign inventories of early variants of the alphabet in the Near East (Haarmann 2010: 81).

And some of the Aegian way of writing obviously found its way into the Greek alphabet. The derivation of most letters of the Greek alphabet from the Phoenician script, has been proved without leaving any doubt (Threatte 1996). What had remained a matter of debate was the origin of the so-called "additional" or "supplementary" letters of the Greek alphabet, and these are phi, psi and khi (xi). "The origins and sound-values of these supplementary letters have not yet been satisfactorily explained, [...]" (Jeffery 1990: 35). These non-Phoenician features of the Greek alphabet were mostly treated as a quantité négligeable. The letters in question were even "[...] considered as unique and secondary Greek creations" (Wachter 1989: 36). The assumption that the additional letters derive from graphical items of the decaying Aegean linear writing is most pervasive since the parallelism of sign forms strikes the eye (figure 7).

Figure 7: The supplementary letters of the Greek alphabet and their equivalents in Aegean linear writing

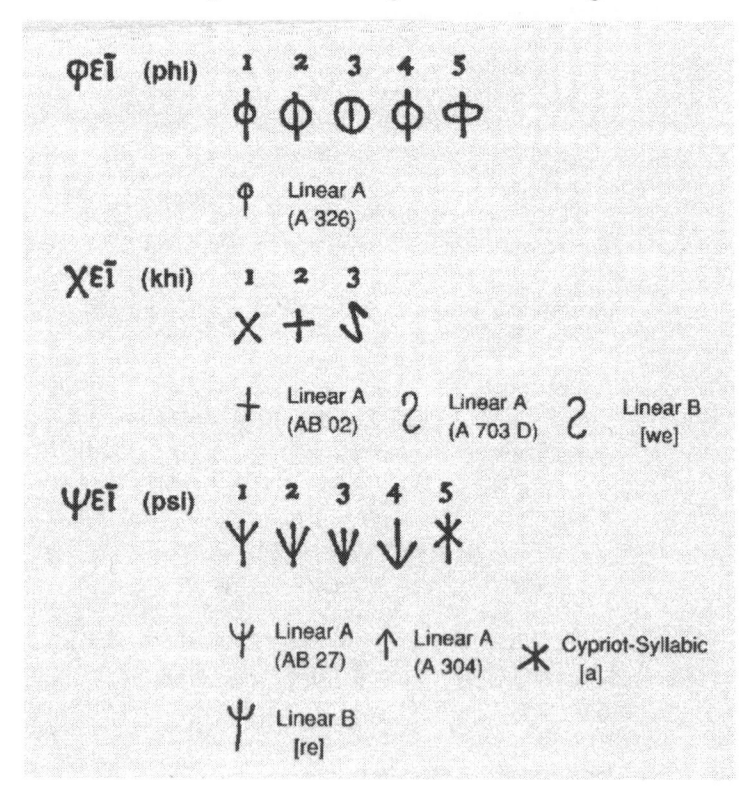

φεῖ (phi)   1 2 3 4 5
ϕ Φ Ⲑ ϕ ⲫ

φ Linear A (A 326)

χεῖ (khi)   1 2 3
Χ + ʃ

+ Linear A (AB 02)   ℩ Linear A (A 703 D)   ℩ Linear B [we]

ψεῖ (psi)   1 2 3 4 5
Ψ ψ ѵ ↓ ✱

ψ Linear A (AB 27)   ↑ Linear A (A 304)   ✱ Cypriot-Syllabic [a]

ψ Linear B [re]

(Haarmann 1995, fig. 170 and 171)

The signs for the supplementary letters are indigenous, but in the sense that they were adopted by the Greeks from their local knowledge of older linear signs, rather than by way of ingenuous "creation". Admittedly, their impact on the formation of the complete Greek alphabet may be minor, but their importance as evidence of pre-Greek literacy, however, makes them significant.

9. Origins of theater as performative art

The world of theater is familiar to all Europeans and, in our cultural vocabulary, we find borrowings from either Greek *theatron* or Latin *theatrum*. As part of the canon of our European education we learn that the ancient Greeks were the first to introduce the theater, including the associated terminology. This view, however, needs to be revised due studies of pre-Greek cultures in the Neolithic and the Bronze Age.

The social interaction of ancient Europeans, descendants of the Old European communities, and ancient Greeks, descendants of Indo-European immigrants to Hellas, the pre-Greek ritual heritage had an impact on the formative process of Greek civilization. Those with roots in Old Europe had continued with certain rituals and festive processions. The general term for 'procession' in ancient Greek is *thiasos*, an expression of pre-Greek origin and rituals are at the very core of the functioning of culture. All cultures of the world, whether historical or recent, operate with behavioral strategies that enhance in-group solidarity, maintain the rigidity of the knowledge obtained from previous generations, and reassure the sustainability of society. "In general a ritual is an act involving performative uses of language (for example, in blessing, praising, cursing, consecrating, purifying) [...] and a formal pattern of behaviour either closely or more loosely followed" (Smart 1997: 72).

There is consensus among scholars that ritual preceded theater, that ritualistic performance provides the mind frame for the reworking of eternal human matters like love, hatred, liberty, power and death projected into the fictional world of theater. If this is true, then it is reasonable to assert that theater is ritualistic healing and that the impression of a play goes far beyond entertainment, for example, with the experience of "drama as therapy" (Jones 1996).

> "Rituals are performative: they are acts done; and performances are ritualized: they are codified, repeatable actions. The functions of theatre identified by Aristotle and Horace – entertainment, celebration, enhancement of social solidarity, education (including political education), and healing – are also functions of ritual. The difference lies in context and emphasis." (Schechner 1994: 613)

The linkage between ritual and theatrical performance in the Greek world has been investigated with some scrutiny (e.g. Kowalzig 2007, Csapo and Miller 2007). However, the historical depth of this linkage has not yet been fully perceived by classical scholars. Some would look for the origins of theatrical performance but, following Vernant and Vidal-Naquet (1990: 23) "it would be better to speak of antecedents".

The symbiotic interplay between drama and ritual can be reconstructed for a world where the early Greeks vividly interacted with the indigene ancient Europeans. Different from the classical era, processions in the archaic period were more comprehensive since they still included theatrical performances in which both men and women participated. Theatrical performances marked the final phase of processions, and it is important to perceive "the position of the 'theatre' as end-point of a procession. The procession was the core of the rural Dionysia, and theatrical performances an addendum" (Wiles 1997: 26).

- **The Old European tradition of theater as performance**

The sixth century BCE saw a breaking away from older ritual traditions and a remodelling of cultural life. The major occurrence was the separation of the theatrical performances from the organization of the processions that continued to be held. The consequences of the separation were of a formal rather than of a contextual nature. The performances remained ritualistic and religiously connotated.

In the early stage of development of theatrical performance, independent of processions, the spoken texts and the scenical arrangements were much simpler than what the Greek theater produced in the classical period. Elaboration and sophistication of language use and narrative lay in the future, with great names such as Aeschylus, Aristophanes, Sophocles and Euripides (Mastromarco and Totaro 2012: 68 ff., 94 ff., 120 ff., 192 ff.).

Even when theatrical performance had been separated from the performance of ritual processions it remained associated with the tradition of mythical narration. The ancient links with ritual processions can be readily identified in the genre of Greek tragedies. Aeschylus who is regarded by many to be the father of European drama carefully preserves the memory of the old roots of Greek theater, that is ritualistic performance of dance and song.

> "Fifth-century Attic tragedy, like archaic epic poetry, took its subjects almost exclusively from myth. Tragedies on nonmythical themes were never more than experimental. [...] Tragedy was also influenced by the treatment of myth in epic poetry. Even ancient authors called Homer the fa-

ther of tragedy, and Aeschylus reportedly said that he worked with the crumbs from Homer's table (TrGF vol. 3, T 112a-b). The tragic poet deliberately situated himself in the epic tradition of mythical narration." (Graf 1993: 142)

The theater as a space with specific functions of performance is a secondary innovation. This can be illustrated by the etymology of the Greek term *theatron*. The stem *thea* points at a word of the pre-Greek substratum, meaning "theatrical performance" (Beekes 2010: 536). The suffix *-tron* (denotating a means for achieving an effect – in this case devising a space for display) was added later, once the architectural form of theaters was introduced. "As a literary genre with its own rules and characteristics tragedy introduces a new type of spectacle into the system of the city-state's public festivals" (Vernant and Vidal-Naquet 1990: 23).

There is an obvious distinction between theater plays as literary works and the theatrical performance of their contents. The reality of cultural life in Athens since the fifth century BCE illustrates a different view. Priority lay with the theatrical performance and theater plays were written to be performed in the theaters that were constructed in Athens and other cities of Attica. One theater stands out because of its unrivaled attraction. "Most, if not all, extant Greek tragedies were written for the Theatre of Dionysus Eleuthereus in Athens" (Wiles 1997: 23). The popularity of theater performances in the ancient Greek world and, in Athens in particular, can hardly be overemphasized.

> "Socrates is reported to have frequently attended the theaters, especially when Euripides competed with new tragedies; when the poet was competing at the Rural Dionysia

in the Piraeus, Socrates even went down there. [...] Beginning in the later fifth century there is evidence for an increasing number of dramatic festivals and theaters across Attica." (Roselli 2011: 21)

– The Greek innovation of theater as architectural form

The layer of pre-Greek terms in the lexical domain of house-construction is extensive. And yet, there are no known borrowings relating to the construction of theaters. This is not surprising since there were no theaters in Greece before the sixth century BCE, and there are no architectural remains of earlier periods that would resemble Greek theaters since there was no need for it according to the traditions of the pre-Greek era.

What is clear is that theatrical performances of Old European traditions continued and received a location in the Greek era. What is not clear is whether the rectangular shape of theaters is older than the theater with a circular space for the audience. In any case, it has been emphasized that the round shape was the preferred model since the fifth century BCE, and this form originated in Athens (Ober 2008: 200 ff.).

The circular shape of the space for the audience offers a practical as well as a symbolic advantage over rectangular constructions. "An inward-facing circle allows maximum eye-contact; each person knows that other people know because each person can visually verify that others are paying attention" (Chwe 2001: 5). Each spectator has a chance, not only to follow how the plot unfolds but to also observe the reactions of other spectators to what happens on the stage. Intervisibility is given priority, not only in the construction of theaters, but also of other public buildings.

> "There is a historical association between democracy in Athens and architecture promoting intervisibility. Like the Greek theater, the *ekklesiasterion* (theater-like public meeting place for gatherings of a city assembly; in Athens, the Pnyx), the *bouleuterion* (large-scale roofed public building for a large probouleutic council), and the *prutanikon* (public building intended for public gatherings of several dozen magistrates; in Athens, the Tholos) may be Athenian architectural innovations." (Ober 2008: 209)

The most perfectioned form of the circular theater is the amphitheater. Most of the amphitheaters of antiquity were constructed by the Romans (Bomgardner 2000). The best-known amphitheater of the Roman world is perhaps the Colosseum in Rome. This monumental building, erected between 72 and 80 CE, ranges among the greatest works of Roman architecture. Those who built the Colosseum were Jewish prisoners of war who had been brought to Italy by Vespasian after his victory over the Jewish army in Iudaea, ending the first Jewish-Roman war.

With the roots of theatrical performance under the auspices of Old European communality the popularity of the theater – as a medium of communal interaction in an environment where ancient traditions were kept up – increased in the course of time, and this can be inferred from the growing capacities to accommodate spectators. The history of the Theater of Dionysus, located on the southern slope of the Acropolis in Athens, is quite informative in this regard. The original version of this particular theater, built in the classical period (fifth century BCE), had seats for some 4,000 spectators while the enlarged version of the Hellenistic era (fourth century BCE) offered space for a maximum of 17,000 spectators (Gogos 2008).

10. The Odyssey: Old European soundings in world literature

The Indo-European migrants who transferred the cult of warrior heroes to the world of Old Europe encountered there another type of hero, the peaceful adventurer. The narrative accounts about the adventures of Odysseus, the protagonist of the *Odyssey*, echo maritime experiences from the world of Old Europe (i.e. shipbuilding and seafaring; Haarmann 2018). When taking into consideration that the origin of the poetic meter, the hexameter, has been identified as dating to pre-Greek times, the Hellenicized fashion of the *Odyssey* reveals its fabric as a sublime case of cultural fusion.

The peaceful hero among the indigenous population, the ancient Europeans, had experienced something that the heroes from the steppe region found attractive, divine patronage. The Indo-European cult of heroes merged with the cult of protective goddesses of Old European descent, in particular with Athena whose cult and name have been identified as of pre-Greek origin (Haarmann 2014: 26 ff.). The fusion of cultural traits enhanced the development of the profile for a new entity, with the Old European legacy merging with Indo-European traditions. It is conclusive to assume that the Old European heritage of oral narrative survived, in whatever transformed way. The fact that elementary symbols of Old Europe did not lose their significance in religious life has been broadly documented (Gimbutas 1989, Haarmann 2014, 2019a). Accordingly, why would elementary themes of the narrative tradition have disappeared without leaving any traces?

But if such narrative elements survived how can we retrieve motifs and narrative patterns of stories which are older than the Indo-European stories about warrior-heroes? In fact, the integration of Old European themes of oral literature into the cycle of epic poetry in the archaic era turns out to be a special showcase of the fusion process, involving the fabric of two divergent cultural mainstreams.

In fact, clues may be found evidencing the connection between epic literature in Greek antiquity and the tradition of story-telling among the people in the Old European civilization. These clues are hidden in the *Odyssey*. The figure of Odysseus is somehow deviant because it does not fit in the patterns of the cult of heroes of Indo-European coinage who are valiant warriors. In the description of environmental specifics (maritime landscapes) where events take place we can distinguish topics and motifs that link the epic story to the distant past, back in time and long before the beginnings of Greek history.

The panorama of clues documenting such linkage is multi-faceted:

(i) Debating Homer's authorship of the *Odyssey*

It is common practice to list the *Odyssey* as one of the epic works of Homer, dating to the eighth century BCE (e.g. Howatson 2011: 403). And yet, consensus regarding Homer's authorship only exists for the other famous work, the *Iliad*, while the role of this poet as author of the *Odyssey* has been a matter of scholarly debate (Graziosi 2002,

Michalopoulos 2016). The alternative option for identification is the assumption that the narrative theme of the seafaring Odysseus had existed before Homer's lifetime and that this poet became attracted to the stories about this figure. The pre-Greek narratives featuring a seafaring protagonist were raised to epical center-stage by Homer's poetic skills (Jensen 1980). And there is evidence supporting the view that the oral-formulaic version of the epic story originated in the pre-Greek era.

(ii) The pre-Greek source for the name of Odysseus

What strikes the modern observer is the plethora of variant forms for this name:

Odysseus, Odyseus (in epic literature),

Olys(s)eus (> Latin Ulysses),

Olyt(t)eus,

Oliseus,

Oulixeus (> Latin Ulyxes)

The derivatives are based on the forms with -d- and -l-: Odysseia "Odyssey" (name of the epic poem), Olisseidai (name of a family in Thebes and Argos).

There have been various attempts to reconstruct an Indo-European root word as source of the name. However, such attempts have remained unsatisfactory and the results have been classified as folk etymology. "The name is typically Pre-Greek [...] on account of the many variants" (Beekes 2010: 1049).

It is noteworthy that also the name of Odysseus' wife, Penelope (Penelopeia), is of pre-Greek origin. It is related to *penelops* "wild goose with coloured neck" (Beekes 2010: 1186). Another pre-Greek name is that of the nymph Calypso, derived from the verb *calypto* (*kalypto*) "cover, hide" (Beekes 2010: 628 f.). Calypso is the one who hides.

(iii) The maritime environment

Odysseus is the protagonist in adventures that relate to seafaring. In the conventional handbooks on maritime trade, on seafaring and colonization in antiquity, the origins of Greek shipbuilding and the sources of technological know-how remain unexplained. Archaeological finds of remainders of Mycenaean ships date to the latter half of the second millennium BCE. There are no earlier finds that would date to the era when the ancestors of the Greeks learned the craft of shipbuilding. Since there are no Semitic loanwords in this domain of ancient Greek the know-how must have come from a source other than the Near East. This ancient source is the language of the traders of Old Europe who had established a network of maritime trade relations already in the fifth millennium BCE, in a period when the ancestors of the Greeks were still living in landlocked communities, in the steppe region.

And so it is not surprising to learn that there is no terminology for ship-building or navigation in the Proto-Indo-European vocabulary. In short, the heroes of the early Indo-Europeans did not embark on maritime voyages simply because their activities were unrelated to the sea. This means that Odysseus could not possibly have been an Indo-European hero of the first day.

Was this figure then a "secondary" hero that originated in the period of Greek colonization along the coasts of the Aegean Sea and the western Mediterranean? No, he wasn't. Instead, there is a connection with the legacy of Old Europe, and there is more to this connection than only the name Odysseus. The earliest layer in the terminology of shipbuilding in ancient Greek is comprised of lexical elements, borrowed from the pre-Greek substrate language (Haarmann 2018). And these borrowings date to the pre-Greek period (see below).

(iv) The pre-Greek sources for the musical instruments of the bards

The terms for the instruments which were used by Homer and other bards in the archaic age, the *kithara* and the *phorminx* (*phormigx*), for the presentation of their epic songs are not Greek. The terms stem from the substrate language and, thus, ultimately derive from the language of the ancient Europeans (Beekes 2010: 694 f., 1587). Since the names of these instruments are pre-Greek, it is most probable that the Greeks adopted the instruments from their predecessors in Hellas, the non-Indo-European population, together with the names and the skills to play them.

(v) The pre-Greek sources for the "Greek" hexameter

The typical literary meter for epic poetry is the hexameter. For the Greek poets applying the rhyme patterns of the hexameter to epic texts was a cumbersome business because this meter does not fit the ancient Greek language well. No need to wonder why this is so. The explanation is simple: the hexameter is not originally Greek but it was adopted from the bards and poets of the pre-Greek age. Before it entered the sphere of Greek culture, the hexameter was applied to a language not akin to Greek (see below).

(vi) The skills of an adventurer vis-à-vis the vicissitudes of life

Odysseus does not fit in the patterns that can be reconstructed for the typical Indo-European heroes. He is no warrior nor is he interested in warfare. Odysseus does not seek fame in fights with enemies. He does not slay neither men nor women just for gaining fame, unlike Achilles in the *Iliad* who kills Hector and Pentiseleia, the queen of the Amazons. Odysseus is no adventurer like Jason, leader of the Argonauts who sets out in search of bounty (i.e. the Golden Fleece). Odysseus is described as a man coping with changing conditions of life and coping with obstacles of all kinds. Thanks to his skills and cleverness Odysseus escapes the nymph who had captured him (i.e. Calypso; *Odyssey*, book 9) and he does not fall victim to the charms of supernatural seductresses, the Sirens (*Odyssey*, book 12).

The lack of militant pride and of egocentric fame-seeking make Odysseus a figure that fits the image of the peace-loving ancient Europeans.

When taking the characteristic deviant features of the *Odyssey* and of its protagonist, Odysseus, into consideration the overall picture of epic poetry of Old European coinage gains in profile. This "deviant" tradition was skilfully adopted by the Greek poets of the archaic age and integrated into their own purely Indo-European repertory of hero stories. Although there were no kings in Old Europe and social hierarchy did not exist, the character of the pre-Greek hero is adapted to social distinctions in Greek society of the archaic age, making him a king (of Ithaka). The result is a symbiotically interwoven organic whole which has come down to us as "Greek" epic poetry but is in the line of continuation from ancient Europe.

– Odysseus and his patron Athena: An intimate companionship

Odysseus is no slayer of monsters but he wounds a monster. According to the mythical account, Odysseus meets the cyclops Polyphemos in a cave where he offers the monster wine to make him drunk and then blinds him with a wooden stake (*Odyssey*, book 9). This is no act of uncontrolled violence carried out by Odysseus but a move to save his companions, who accompany Odysseus on his voyages. Without the intervention of Odysseus the cyclops would have devoured his ship's crew members. The cyclops is the son of Poseidon, god of the sea. Poseidon gets enraged and his mind is clouded by aspirations to take revenge for the harm Odysseus has done to Polyphemus. On the god's behalf Odysseus is prevented from returning to his home in Ithaka for ten years. During this time, he has to endure hardship of all kind:

> "For his sake Poseidon, shaker of the earth, although he does not kill Odysseus, yet drives him back from the land of his fathers." (*Odyssey*, book 1.74)

It turns out that Athena, the patron goddess, becomes the closest companion for Odysseus. The goddess herself explains her preference to function as a guardian for the hero:

> "We both know tricks, since you [Odysseus] are by far the best among all men in counsel and tales, but I among all the Gods have renown for wit [*metis*] and tricks." (*Odyssey*, book 13: 360-362)

King Nestor, an attentive observer, makes an insightful comment on the relationship between Odysseus and Athena:

> "[…] for I never saw the Gods showing such open affection as Pallas Athena stood by him for all to see."
> (*Odyssey*, book 3: 214)

Throughout the accounts about happenings in the *Odyssey*, Athena takes the role of a messenger and mediator, and only on rare occasions does the goddess intervene in concrete action (e.g. when Odysseus and Telemachus fight with the suitors in book 22). Athena is not only the companion of Odysseus, and his guardian, but she is empathic also with his family members, with Telemachus, the son of Odysseus, and with Penelope, his wife. This feature of character, empathy and compassion, makes Athena's companionship with Odysseus so very special. One may even advocate the idea that Athena is a protagonist of the *Odyssey* on equal terms with her companion. Reference to Athena in the *Odyssey* is made 162 times (see George 1999 for an overview of citations).

− The topic of peace as common good

The role of Athena as peace-maker deserves special attention:

> "And now would they [Odysseus and his son Telemachus] have slain them [the treacherous suitors] all, and cut them off from returning, had not Athena, daughter of Zeus, who

bears the aegis, shouted aloud, and checked all the host, saying: „Refrain, men of Ithaca, from grievous war, that with all speed you may part, and that without bloodshed." (*Odyssey*, book 24.529-532)

"Then flashing-eyed Athena spoke to Odysseus saying: „Son of Laertes, sprung from Zeus, Odysseus of many devices, stay thy hand, and make the strife of equal war to cease, lest haply the son of Cronos be wroth with thee, even Zeus, whose voice is borne afar." (*Odyssey*, book 24.533-544)

"So spoke Athena, and he obeyed, and was glad at heart. Then for all time to come a solemn covenant betwixt the twain was made by Pallas Athena, daughter of Zeus, who bears the aegis, in the likeness of Mentor both in form and in voice." (*Odyssey*, book 24.545-548)

It is in the *Odyssey* that the topic of peace-making is addressed whereas there is no mention at all of any peace-making arranged by the goddess in the *Iliad*. In the *Iliad*, peace comes with the Achaian Greeks having achieved victory over the Trojans, that is with one of the warring parties left as losers of the conflict. When Athena declares peace in the *Odyssey* this means concluding peace among equals with the demand of abstaining from further armed confrontation. Here, the goddess takes the role of a guarantor of peace.

Such conditions of peace-restoring under divine surveillance recall the spirit of life conduct in Old Europe. For the ancient Europeans, peaceful community life ranged among the basic values. Whatever conflict might have occurred, the ancient Europeans trusted in the authority and blessing of the goddess for peaceful conditions to be restored. So it is not surprising that the Greeks adopted the expression for the key concept 'peace' from the language of their predecessors: *eirene* (Beekes 2010: 391).

In the awareness that the figure of Odysseus, the theme of seafaring and the poetic recording of epic stories in the hexameter have pre-Greek origins, the assumption seems conclusive that the exceptional affection of the goddess Athena as patron – in light of her divine pre-Greek genealogy – may ultimately be motivated by the intrinsic linkage of hero and goddess with the same cultural milieu, the world of Old Europe.

11. Seafaring and shipbuilding: The longevity of Old European expertise

Seafaring and navigation were alien to the Proto-Indo-European pastoralists in the steppe. Therefore, it is obvious that stories about maritime adventures like those presented in the *Odyssey* could not possibly have originated among the landlocked pastoralist communities. But does this mean that the adventures of Odysseus are a theme that emerged as late as the period when the descendants of the Indo-European migrants had settled Hellas, that is in the second millennium BCE? On the contrary, the theme of the *Odyssey* is much older and is associated with the era when the ancient Europeans practised seafaring and navigated the Aegean Sea, the Ionian Sea and other parts of the Mediterranean, and also the waters along the western litoral of the Black Sea.

In all probability, Odysseus is a figure that was created by bards in the world of Old Europe. Reference to seafaring, shipbuilding and navigation is made about 400 times in the *Odyssey*, and among the terminology used are elements of the oldest layer of loanwords in ancient Greek, of pre-Greek origin.

After the ancestors of the Greeks had arrived in the south and had begun settling down they got to know an environment that was strange in the first place because the newcomers had not have any experience with marine conditions. The indicator that reflects the early Greeks' lack of experience is their language. The newcomers learned many words from the natives for phenomena that they did not know, starting with the most general expression for a marine environment, *thalassa* (with a variant *thalatta*). This expression which has survived to this day in modern Greek is the word for "sea". *Thalassa* is not related to any of the inherited expressions for sea in Indo-European languages. The original inland orientation of the early migrants is „supported by the fact that those stocks actually living adjacent to an open sea (e.g., the Greeks, the Germans and the Indo-Aryans) had borrowed words for the body of water from non-IE sources, e.g., Grk *thalatta* 'sea', OE *sæ* 'sea' (> NE *sea*), Goth *saiws* 'sea'" (Mallory and Adams 1997: 503).

After the ancestors of the Greeks had arrived in the south and had begun settling down they got to know an environment that was strange in the first place because the newcomers had not have any experience with marine conditions. The indicator that reflects the early Greeks' lack of experience is their language. The newcomers learned many words from the natives for phenomena that they did not know, starting with the most general expression for a marine environment, *thalassa* (with a variant *thalatta*). This expression which has survived to this day in modern Greek is the word for "sea". *Thalassa* is not related to any of the inherited expressions for sea in Indo-European languages. The original inland orientation of the early migrants is "supported by the fact that those stocks actually living adjacent to an open sea (e.g., the Greeks, the Germans and the Indo-Aryans) had borrowed words for the body of water from non-IE sources, e.g., Grk *thalatta* 'sea', OE *sæ* 'sea' (> NE *sea*), Goth *saiws* 'sea'" (Mallory and Adams 1997: 503).

By the time when the Mycenaean Greeks entered the competition of maritime trade with the Phoenicians, the technology and terminology of shipbuilding among the Greeks had already been well-established. The Greeks continued a legacy of seafaring that had persisted since the era when the Old European civilization flourished in southeastern Europe, during the Neolithic and Copper Age.

The tradition of pre-Greek seafaring in the ancient Aegean has been associated with the narrative canon in the Odyssey (Watrous 2007). In the wall-paintings of Akrotiri (ancient Thera, modern Santorini) – above all in the scenes of the "flotilla fresco" – we find vivid illustrations of ships moving in a ritual maritime procession (Doumas 1992: 68-83).

It is often claimed that the Greeks learned the know-how of shipbuilding from the Phoenicians. If this were true one would expect a considerable layer of Semitic loanwords in this lexical domain of ancient Greek. And yet, "none of the words for parts of ships in Greek derives from a Semitic root" (Hall 2014: 12). Furthermore, at the time when the ancient Greeks had learned to build ships and started to explore the coastal waters there had been no contact between the Greek mainland and Egypt. Also, the Near Eastern connection is not valid. But we know, that the shipbuilding skills in the other ancient civilizations (i.e. Egypt, Mesopotamia) developed much later.

Some of the useful know-how of Old European shipbuilders found its way – through manifold transformations – into Greek craftsmanship, and some technical terms of the pre-Indo-European substrate language survived in the specialized vocabulary of ancient Greek (according to the entries in Beekes' *Etymological dictionary*, 2010):

– parts of the ship

aphlaston "curved poop of a ship, with its ornaments" (cf. the decorated sterns of ancient Cycladic boats; Bintliff 2011: 105), *boutani* "part of the ship to which the rudder is tied", *kanthelia* "curved pieces of wood at the back of a ship", *kindynos* "bench in the prow of a ship", *lenos* "socket into which the mast fitted", *selis* "crossbeam of a ship", *stamines* "vertical side-beams of a ship", *halkes* "board, rib of a ship", etc.

– parts of the equipment of the ship

agkyra "anchor", *eune* "anchor stones", *laipha / laiphe* "sail made of skin", *sipharos* "topsail, topgallant sail"

– material for shipbuilding

kalon "wood for building ships", *malthe* "mix of wax and pitch, used to caulk ships", *ptakana* "boat mat (used in boats called *kanna*)"

– terminology relating to seafaring

kybernao "to steer (a ship)"

It is from the Mycenaean era that we find the earliest mention of the profession of "shipbuilders" (*naudomoi*, written as na-u-do-mo in the Linear B texts, derived from *naus* "ship"). Other terms referring to seafaring are "rowers, oarsmen" (*eretai*, written as e-re-ta in Mycenaean texts) and "sailor, mariner" (*pontilos*, as po-ti-ro in Linear B). Also various personal names, recorded in Mycenaean texts, are derived from the stem *naus*: e.g. O-ti-na-wo (Ortinawos),

Na-u-si-ke-re-we (Nausiklewes "One who is famous because of his ships"), Na-wi-ro (Nawilos "Sailor"), O-ku-na-wo (Okunawos "Someone possessing a fast ship"), E-u-o-mo (Euhormos "Someone possessing a good harbor"); (Ilievski 2000: 364, 369).

The Mycenaeans did not only built ships for trade but they also to wage war. The most famous of those wars for strengthening Mycenaean political power in the region was the Trojan war whose agents, the heroes of the Trojans and the Achaians, gained immortality in Homer's epic work *Iliad*.

To gain influence and political power may have been the reason for the Mycenaeans to established settlements outside the Greek mainland i.e. on the Ionian coast of the Aegean, in Asia Minor. Mycenaean merchants explored the sea route to the west and founded trading-posts in southern Italy. Remains of Mycenaean pottery are relics of that time.

Human genetic research has produced evidence that the ancestors of the Etruscans came from the northern part of the Aegean Sea and frequented the sea routes that had been established by Mycenaean seafarers (Haarmann 2019c: 56 ff.). In the vocabulary of Etruscan one finds elements of terminology of shipbuilding that are borrowed from the Old European language, terms that find their equivalents in the layer of lexical borrowings in ancient Greek (see in the foregoing). It is no exaggeration to claim that the tradition of seafaring and shipbuilding, introduced by the Etruscans to Italy, is a reflection of longevity of navigational skills of Old European coinage.

With the newly gained knowhow the ancient Greeks were prepared for their mercantile endeavors in the areas surrounding the Mediterranean and the Black Sea, and in the antique sources we find much information about how they conducted business with other Greeks and with foreigners. Greeks had begun to found colonies abroad already during the "dark ages". The first to start the colonial enterprise were the Spartans who established a trading center on the Cycladic island of Thera (modern Santorini) around 1000 BCE (Osborne 1996: 121).

> "The constant and close reliance on the sea, and on the ships that sailed it, could not have failed to influence the language of the ancient Greeks, the metaphors and pictures in which their ideas were expressed. The result is that passages of Greek poetry and prose writing are often inscrutable without a knowledge of the nautical practice which lies behind them, and modern ignorance has led on occasion to corruption of the text." (Morrison and Williams 1968: 1)

People of Old Europe settling on the territory of nowadays Greece had shared their expertise with Indo-European newcomers to the region, ancestors of the Greeks, and the transfer of knowledge and terminology relating to seafaring became an important piece in the mosaic of Greek culture.

12. The hexameter and its pre-Greek origin

In the beginning, stories about heroes were told to selected crowds by trained narrators (bards), and the narrative expression did not lose its importance at the time when those stories were recorded in writing. The written form was just another media to convey the contents of epic stories.

The situation of the narrator who went from town to town, being invited to the homes of noblemen to entertain the guests at banquets is described in the *Odyssey* (book 8.62-73) where the blind poet (i.e. Homer) is escorted into the banquet hall and asked to perform:

> "And the herald approached, leading the honored poet
> whom the Muse loved beyond all others, granting him both
> good and evil: she deprived him of sight but gave him
> the gift of sweet song. The herald, Pontonous,
> set out for him a large chair, studded with silver,
> in the midst of the banquet and leaned it against a tall pillar,
> and he hung the beautiful clear-toned lyre on a peg
> a little above the singer's head, and he showed him
> how to reach up and take hold of it in his hands.
> And he put on a table beside him a basket of food
> and a cup of wine to drink when he felt the urge to.
> And they all reached out for the feast that was set before them.
> And when they had enough of eating and drinking,
> the Muse moved the poet to sing of the glorious deeds
> of heroes."

> "No image for the process of composing or enacting a poem is as common as that of a journey, sometimes, [...], a flight above the earthbound, pedestrian (*pezos*) world of prose. The idea is strikingly thematised in the *Argonautica* of Apollonius Rhodius in which, as has been well recognised, the wanderings of the heroes are overtly linked to the wandering paths of song and the narrator almost travels as an extra Argonaut himself." (Hunter and Rutherford 2009a: 7 f.)

The language of the ancient Europeans provided the many pre-Greek elements that we find, as items of the substratum, in the vocabulary of ancient Greek as well as in personal, tribal and geographical names. Borrowed are also the names for the instruments which were used by Homer and other bards in the archaic age, the *kithara* and the *phormigx*. Since the names of these instruments are pre-Greek, it is most probable that the Greeks adopted the instruments from the Pelasgians, together with the names and the skills to play them.

This raised the question whether the tradition of oral poetry also is pre-Greek. The most popular meter of Greek epic poetry, the hexameter. Criteria for identifying the origin of the hexameter come from within the tradition of Greek literacy, of early poetic language in particular. Findings in the comparative study of local Indo-European literary traditions point to similarities, on the one hand, and to isolated phenomena in Greek poetic patterns, on the other. Similarities have been observed when comparing the line pattern of eleven syllables in the poems of the Greek poetess Sappho, from Lesbos, and in the Rig Veda, first noticed by Antoine

Meillet in his seminal work *Introduction à l'étude comparative des langues indo-européennes* (1937). Within the Greek poetic tradition, Sappho's pattern corresponded to a certain genre of poetry from which the other genre, the epic style, deviated.

> "The Sapphic line characterized the so-called Aeolic poetry. It is important to note that both single [...] and double [...] short can come in between the long syllables. In the Homeric hexameter, to take another case, this is not so. There it is possible for two shorts to take the place of one long syllable (isochronism), something which does not occur in Aeolic or Old Indic poetry. Meillet for this reason wondered whether the hexameter had been borrowed from non-Indo-European inhabitants of Greece." (Beekes 2011: 44)

Inspecting the formulaic pattern of the hexameter in relation to the linguistic structures of the Greek language, this meter is somehow awkward, as if it does not really fit the syllable patterns of ancient Greek. Why would the Greeks have chosen a highly complex meter as a vehicle for oral poetry? A much simpler medium would have served the purpose, as in the case of other cultures with rich traditions of oral poetry.

It is demonstrated that the Hexameter was not developed by Greek poets (C.J. Ruijgh 1988). It had existed in pre-Mycenaean times, that is in Minoan literary tradition of ancient Crete. No extant epic literature of Minoan has come down to us but the allusions in antique sources make it highly probable that such a literary genre once flourished in ancient Crete.

The proto-Greeks brought an ancient poetic language variety for recording myths, evidenced by Beekes (2011: 42 f.), with them and, in the course of contacts with the ancient Europeans with their own mythic tradition and metrical forms, the early Greeks adopted the originally non-Greek meter to give their epic language a formulaic framework. Mycenaean civilization played a pivotal role for the continuity of myths and legends about the heroic deeds of the ancestors. After the decline of the Mycenaeans' political power, the cultural memory of the golden age of Mycenaean society did not vanish but rather its contents was transformed, in the intergenerational chain, to assume mythopoetic proportions.

> "Greek epic poetry about legendary persons from Mycenaean times grew in the same way as did folk songs about mediaeval heroes in the Balkan countries during the Turkish domination. Greek legends were especially vivid among the descendants of those Mycenaean families who escaped the Dorian violence and emigrated to the Aegean islands and to Asia Minor. Homesick for their mother country, they did not forget the famous leaders and founders of their cities and colonies. These heroic legends became the base of the Homeric poems which glorify the brave Achaeans, i.e. Mycenaeans." (Ilievski 2000: 371)

The hexameter is not the only poetic meter that the Greeks adopted from their predecessors in Hellas. Another popular meter is the iambus, and this is also of pre-Greek origin (Beekes 2010: 572). All in all, the awareness of the great age of the cult of heroes and of stories crystallizing around mythical figures bears witness to how firmly the epic genre and its metrical form had permeated Greek culture long before its height in the classical age.

13. The findings of Marija Gimbutas focusing on migration – Contours of a differential typology

It is among the merits of the eminent scholar Marija Gimbutas to have outlined the contours of major movements of ancient ethnic groups that changed the demographic structures and the genetic profile of populations in Europe in the course of several millennia (from the fifth through the second millennium BCE). These movements have become known as Kurgan migrations or out-migrations from the Eurasian steppe, respectively. For decades, the concept of migrations was a matter of dispute, with Renfrew's hypothesis of Indo-European migration from Anatolia into Europe in opposition to the Kurgan model. In his memorable speech at the Oriental Institute in Chicago, in November 2017, Colin Renfrew put an end to the debate by acknowledging the timeless validity of the migration concept of Marija Gimbutas:

> "Her Kurgan invasion theory was viewed with reservations by several scholars, yet recent work on ancient DNA has given strong support to her views and brought them back into prominence"
> (see the website of the Institute of Archaeomythology for details; <www.archaeomythology.org>).

In light of such prominent vindication one would expect a turn toward unanimity in those circles where research on migrations and their aftereffects are relevant, above all in the archaeology of ancient European history. Yet, there are still scholars who adhere to the outdated rejection of the Kurgan model or who have not yet become aware of the magnitude of those population movements. In his assessment of demic diffusion in connection with the development of agrarian lifeways in Europe, Bar-Yosif (2017: 315) speaks of "additional dispersals" from the steppe, as if this were of minor importance, obviously ignorant of the magnitude of the third major movement of populations from the steppe (Kurgan III) that has been identified by human geneticists as „massive migrations" (Haak et al. 2015).

One would also think that, in light of the re-appraisal of the model of Kurgan migrations, scholars would rethink their previous criticism of the migration concept and pay due attention to the lucid description by Marija Gimbutas of how the movements were motivated, how they unfolded and how they brought about change for the communities of local populations, in southeastern Europe, in particular. However, inconceivable criticism is still retained by some scholars. For instance, in his comment on the Kurgan model, David Anthony (2022) states: "[…] it is an exaggeration to say that she [Marija Gimbutas] was right. We need to move beyond the single-event, invasion model of migration and accept the much more complex models that historians and demographers use to model migrations […]". This comment is misleading.

Evidently, it has escaped this critic that Marija Gimbutas, in her germinal publications, did not present a "single-event, invasion model" but instead provided a differential model of migrations from the steppe (see below). It is somehow ironical that it is exactly the abandoned hypothesis of Anatolian origins, the model long propagated by Colin Renfrew which has produced an undifferentiated pattern of migration of the spread of the agrarian package via migration of farmers from Anatolia to southeastern Europe. According to the model of Anatolian origins of agriculture the agrarian package was brought to continental Europe by farmers from Anatolia who did not interact with the locals but allegedly drove the indigenous foragers away and established their own settlements. In light of this simplistic model of colonization, agrarian lifeways spread with genetically Anatolian farmers in southeastern Europe.

Yet, such an undifferentiated scenario cannot be corroborated by modern genetic investigations. On the contrary, insights from recent interdisciplinary studies speak in favour of a dynamic process of acculturation involving the indigenous population, so that the former foragers adopted agrarian lifeways themselves. Though initially inspired by pioneer groups of farmers from Anatolia, most of the spread of the agrarian package in Greece and the Balkanic region is the result of local acculturation processes. Those who had acculturated and shifted to a sedentary way of life took the lead in the unfolding of agrarian community life in southeastern Europe. There is a visionary consequence of these findings. Those who were foremost responsible for modulating the fabric of the hub of Old Europe were indigenous people, the ancient Europeans.

There is good reason to contrast the simplistic model of Anatolian migrations into Europe with the differential model of Indo-European migrations under the impression of which the Old European heritage became transformed. In this connection, it is essential to highlight some of the major aspects of this differential model, the Kurgan model elaborated by Marija Gimbutas, to demonstrate its applicability and continuing usefulness, as a tool for modern investigations.

– Multifaceted motivations for migration

The movements of pastoralists from the Eurasian steppe into other parts of Europe were not random. Such movements were repetitive and, it is noteworthy that they were neither organized according to a uniform pattern, nor were they similarly motivated. A broad panorama of pertinent motivations was responsible for triggering individual migrations.

As a result of long term trade contacts of ancient Europeans travelling to the steppe to exchange goods with with Indo-European steppe pastoralists the potential for conflict between the two groups remained minimal, despite fundamental contrasts in the structuring of their community life and worldview. The balance of peaceful trade relations shifted to a scenario of conflict around 4600 /4500 BCE in the north east when first small groups of Indo-Europeans moved from the steppe into the aera of Old European settlements (Kurgan IThe movement from the steppe increased with the second out-migration (Kurgan II) from the steppe which penetrated further into Old European territory in the time span between 4100 and 3800 BCE. and, with the third and biggest wave of immigration of Indo-Europeans in the time span between 3200 and 2800 BCE (Kurgan III) which became fatal for the integrity of Old European culture (see Haarmann and LaBGC 2021 for an outline).

Each of the three movements were set in motion by a specific pattern of motivation for each – and each of the three movements in turn triggered migrations by displacing Old Europeans from their ancestral territories (see below). In order to perceive the scale and magnitude of each movement it is important to distinguish the various factors that had an impact on how migration was motivated and, eventually, triggered. The interplay of relevant factors that contributed to the overall process of migration can be specified as follows:

(i) environmental change and its effect on living-conditions

- climate change was continuous and at times dramatic from the Palaeolithic throughout antiquity; see Anderson et al. 2007, Burroughs 2005, Haarmann 2020 and Radoane 2021 for changing conditions in the region north of the Black Sea;

- conditions of the „Atlantic period" with its humid and warm climate, c. 6900-3800 BCE;

- the emergence of the Black Sea as the outcome of a catastrophic event ("the Black Sea Flood") and the inundation of vast areas around the former Euxine Lake around 6400 BCE (see Ryan and Pitman 1998, Haarmann 2003, Marler and Haarmann 2006, Brukner 2006 on the consequences of this catastrophic event on the ecological conditions of the wider region), causing pressure on native ancient Europeans to found new settlements in regions not afflicted by inundations;

- a rapid cooling around the Black Sea and in the Eurasian steppe due to the "8 ka cold event" (Budja 2007);

- a rapid warming around 5800 BCE;

Climate-induced environmental changes have caused patterns of great variability and contrast in the living-conditions of the steppe zone that originated after the end of the last ice age. Contrasts between warm and cold, wet and dry with varying spans of duration for differing stages raised the level of changeability of living-conditions among human beings and their herds. The readiness to keep up mobility was essential for communal cohesiveness among pastoralists living in the steppe zone and decisively shaped their mindset. In combination with other factors (see factors listed under ii – vi) this readiness for mobility eventually spurred collective movements among clans of pastoralists in the steppe, culminating in the documented out-migrations of Indo-Europeans around 4500 BCE (see below).

(ii) Needs of pastoral economy

– the availability of pastures for the herds;
– the intention and/or need to expand the area of pastures for the cattle;

(iii) The strife for access to natural resources interest in specific resources outside the range of pastoral life (e.g. salt in the region of Provadia in Bulgaria);

(iv) Social reasons

- e.g., the formation of new groups with chief and warriors, demanding new territory for control;

(v) Intensification of trade relations

– a growing interest in trade goods and their distribution (e.g. trade activity in the eastern Cucuteni area);

(vi) Interest in the control of a lucrative trade market (e.g. the trade center at Varna);

(vii) Technological innovation (i.e. wheel and wagon) facilitating the movement of people and goods.

The potential factors for motivation to leave territory in the steppe as listed in the overview (i – vi) become selectively activated and show variability in their significance for the unfolding of migration movements during a certain period. In a historical perspective, we can observe that the motivations for each of the three out-migrations of Indo-Europeans from the steppe were manifold which means that the triggering of movements did not depend on one factor only. Instead, it was always the interplay of various factors that eventually culminated in the movement of small groups or larger parts of the population, depending on the dynamics of the interplay. That is: Indo-Europeans were moving into territory of ancient Europe causing changes for social life of the indigenous population, from an egalitarian system to a hierarchal patriarchal one in order to gain and secure control which caused Old Europeans unwilling to surrender to the change to abandon their territories and migrate to regions where Indo-Europeans were not yet in charge.

The multifaceted scenarios of migration movements from the Eurasian steppe into other parts of Europe, outlined by Marija Gimbutas, have been basically convalidated by continuous research since the 1990s, producing ever more details and confirming the overall validity of the framework of Kurgan migrations and the significance of multiple motivation for mobility. Since the motivation for each out-migration shows a specific pattern, it is conclusive that, due to differences in scale and scope, also the effects of the various migrations show remarkable differences. In the following, the multifaceted scenarios of Kurgan migrations, as outlined by Marija Gimbutas and corroborated by ongoing research, will be examined.

- **Conditions for migration motivated by intentions to control a lucrative trade market (Kurgan I)**

Through trading activities carried out by people from the Danube civilization with the early Indo-European pastoralists in eastern Europe a trading network had been established that reached far beyond the core area of Old European settlements (see map 1 in the Introduction).

In her assessment of the sociopolitical changes that occurred on the eastern periphery of Old Europe in the fifth millennium BCE, Gimbutas (1991: 338) gives the following explanation: "I consider this change a result of rapidly rising trade activities of the inhabitants of the Black Sea coast with the Dnieper-Volga steppe population who were wedging their way into territories west of the Black Sea". This movement, directed toward the trade center of Varna, triggered the first out-migration (Kurgan I).

Varna on the eastern periphery of Old Europe (founded in the early fifth millennium BCE) is a special case among Neolithic settlements in that it developed a vibrant economy and attracted people throughout the region. Located pivotally at the intersection of a trade route over land and a maritime trade route along the western coast of the Black Sea, Varna held a key position as a trade center, connecting the settlements in the south (of the regional Karanovo culture) with those in the north (of the regional Cucuteni and Trypillya cultures).

All the commodities that were produced by craftswomen and craftsmen in the workshops of the economic centers of Old Europe were transported and offered along the eastern trade route: flint blades, artifacts such as rings and beads made of spondylus, small stone axes, metal objects etc. Copper had been worked before 6000 BCE in the form of cold-hammering. Having been developed around 5400 BCE in southern Serbia (according to finds at the sites of Rudna Glava and Belovode), the craft of smelting copper spread rapidly across the economic zone of Old Europe, and objects made of copper are among the trade goods that passed through Varna (map 3). Gold was also traded, and this innovation was introduced a short time before Indo-European pastoralists set out to establish their elite power at Varna.

Map 3:   Varna and its hinterland in the fifth millennium BCE

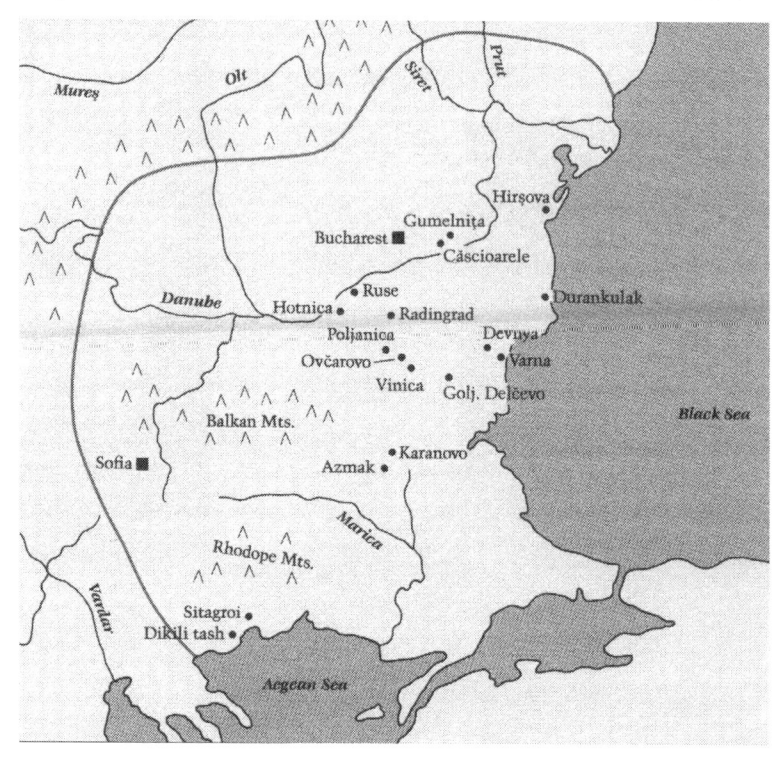

(Gimbutas 1991: 92)

Certain artifacts produced by the ancient Danubians have been found as far east as the Volga basin (Anthony 2009a: 38). Among the finds are breastplates, which became items of prestige among the steppe people. The pastoralists were certainly impressed when getting to know goods they had never seen before and discovering the value of metal objects. The ancient Danubians offered metal tools, but the warriors among the steppe people may have felt inspired by the idea to produce weapons from metal. And so in addition to the constant need to find new pastureland there was another reason why to turn westward where the people of Old Europe lived and obviously prospered.

And another sought after product was available in Varna. The people in the region of Varna had access to a resource that was in short supply elsewhere: salt. Archaeological investigations carried out since 2005 have uncovered a salt-production site at Tell Provadia-Solnitsata, some 6 km southeast of the town of Provadia (Varna District), on the Provadia plateau. Analyses of large vessels used for „dry-boiling" salt water that was collected from salt springs nearby puts the date for the beginning of salt production in the region at c. 5400 BCE, which makes this site the earliest center for the production of salt in all of Europe (Nikolov 2008).

The wealth of Varna as a trade center and the presence of prestige goods there, in particular, may have tipped the scales and after some time the steppe people set out to take influence and to seek control over the region. How did they manage to achieve that goal? There is evidence for the presence of steppe nomads in the Varna region around 4500 BCE. But since there are no signs of destruction at Varna for that time it can be assumed that the takeover by steppe nomads was not hostile. And why should they seek destructive confrontation? It would have been to the detriment of the immigrants who wanted to benefit from both, the technological know-how of the old-established communities and their wealth. The question remains: how did the steppe people gain control?

Most certainly, one factor was the peaceful attitude of the inhabitants of Varna. Why should a community without experience of hostile behaviour and destruction have been suspicious when people from the steppe whom they traded with wanted to settle in Varna? It is easy to imagine that, being certainly proud of their prospering town, they rather welcomed the groups from the north east. And there might have been another factor for unhesitating acceptance of the newcomers. The ancient Danubians may have gazed at the horse-riding lot with admiration. So far they had only heard of horses described by the traders who had seen these animals on their tours to the Indo-Europeans. But in those days, horses were not known in Old Europe.

Life in Varna, as in other communities throughout Old Europe, was built on trust, that we can assume. Had they not trusted each other, their communities would not have thrived the way they did and they would not have remained stable. They would have needed walls to protect their settlements. They would have needed warriors and weapons. None of this was found in Old Europe before the intrusion of Indo-Europeans. Certainly, they had a system to handle conflicts between individuals and groups. This system was the 'municipal council' in each local settlement. The name for such a settlement in the language of the ancient Danubians has survived as a lexical borrowing in ancient Greek: *kome* as described in chapter 3.

How could the inhabitants of Varna with their orientation at the Common Good suspect the coming reversal of values which had been their natural orientation for communal interaction for generations? Quite differently, the people from the steppe. For generations they had experienced hierarchy as helpful for their way of life and therefore accepted orders from their leaders without discussion. These leaders were used to quick assessment of changing situations. For example, in case of rivalries with neighboring clans, that is in situations where the clan leader had to make a stand how to handle the conflict, the option was available to fight immediately without hesitation.

They could rely on their warriors and expect them to obey orders instantly. Accustomed to the hierarchical organization of clan life the pastoralists took advantage of the admiration they met with the locals and of the communal structure of the *kome* in each district of Varna by presenting themselves as helpful and trustworthy new members of the community. When the warriors on horseback showed up, this sufficed to underscore the combat potential that the pastoralists had on their side. Since open conflict was useless, the locals accommodated to the changing conditions, now favouring co-existence under the political leadership of the newcomers.

The graves of people who had died during the political change give important clues. The Neolithic (Copper Age) cemetery at Varna is among the largest known from prehistory, and its hundreds of graves contain a vast amount of artifacts and information about communal life and the social status of the individuals who were interred there. Among the most sensational finds of the Varna necropolis were objects made of gold, the oldest in the world, predating Egyptian or Mesopotamian gold artifacts by at least two thousand years.

The distribution of gold objects in the graves at the Varna cemetery proves that this metal was a prestigious item among the newly established elite of steppe pastoralists. For the first time in the history of burial culture, there was a clear distinction between graves richly equipped with goods and other graves which contained only a few objects of less material value. The arrangement of graves in the cemetery and the distribution of grave goods testify to the emergence of a society stratified with classes and to differences in social status, with an elite ruling over the general populace.

Accordingly, the appearance of gold objects at other places can be interpreted as evidence of the spread of the elite system of political control, in which the ruling minority used visual signifiers (i.e. scepters as status symbols) to ritualize its power over local agriculturalists, craftswomen and craftsmen and traders who experienced a shift from egalitarian to stratified society. The Varna cemetery „illustrates the early stage of the emergence of a class-segregated society, [...] (Slavchev 2009: 203).

The Varna graves point to the earliest manifestation of weaponry as status symbols for a ruling class. The abundance of copper axes in the graves of the Varna Necropolis is a striking feature. It was previously unknown in the burial culture of Old Europe for the grave goods in a single grave to include a multitude of axes, as was the case with graves of males at Varna (figure 8)

Figure 8: Copper axes from the Varna Necropolis

(Slavchev 2009: 201)

The majority of the axes are of copper, which underscores the importance which this type of artifact had to the deceased during his lifetime. Along with finds of axes, a number of spearheads made of copper have been found. It can be reasonably concluded that the abundance of weapons made of metal reflect the zeitgeist of an early warrior elite. The weapons have been understood as "an indication of how control was maintained by the elite and a direct testament to the connection between power and military leadership" (Slavchev 2009: 206).

The Varna cemetery also provides information about the relationship between the new ruling class and the old-established local population. Archeological finds prove the differences.

Before the leaders from the steppe installed themselves and their hierarchical system at Varna the graves in the regions of the Danube civilization had not shown any distinction between poor and rich; the grave goods were equally distributed without any hint on social classes. There was no distinction between the status of men and women, except for a few women whose graves contained more grave goods than the usual ones did. These women might have had highly valued qualities such as in the domain of healing or spirituality. What also had not been found in the graves of Old Europe were regalia insignia such as scepters or artifacts having a heraldic-symbolic function that would identify the deceased as ruler or as belonging to a leading clan (LaBGC & Haarmann 2019).

The graves of the ancient Danubians contained the remains of a single deceased person, either male or female. However, among the graves of the rich in the Varna necropolis, there are some in which members of both sexes are buried. The grave goods of the male exhibit the typical signifiers of steppe culture (i.e. metal axes, symbolic items demonstrating elite status), while the grave goods of the female are typical of Old Europe before the takeover (i.e. female figurines, spindle whorls).

The existence of items in graves of the rich associated with both cultures, that of Old Europe and that of the pastoralists, suggests that leaders of the steppe people married women from the community where they assumed power as rulers, thus establishing ethnically mixed marriages. In this way, members of the local population were incorporated into the ruling elite through intermarriage. The phenomenon of interethnic marriages became a vehicle for promoting sociocultural change and at the same time erasing possible resistance on the side of locals in the community. Step by step the society with orientation at the Common Good and gender equality experienced a transformation toward a patriarchal system with leadership as a claim without contradiction. The system that ensured survival in the steppes, chiefdom, had been transferred to a new environment, and this system, initially forced upon the local population, came to dominate social relations in the intergenerational chain.

In the case of the takeover of the Varna trade center by steppe pastoralists and their warrior elite it is not far-fetched to assume that the leader of the clan assumed power as king-priest and the head of the band of warriors assumed power as head of the king's security forces, and both married women from local families to reinforce relations between migrant-newcomers and local people.

– **Conditions for migration triggering the second out-migration (Kurgan II)**

The Varna takeover during the first outmigration from the steppe (Kurgan I) was peaceful though enforced under the impression of potential threat exerted by the presence of a warrior elite. This attitude of the pastoralists to take control without any escalated conflict seems to have prevailed already prior to the Varna takeover when Indo-Europeans started to intrude into the lands of agriculturalists in the regional Trypillya culture: "[…] the chiefs who migrated from the steppe did not intend to destroy the Trypillya culture, but rather to participate in and control it. The introduction of the chiefdom system into the Trypillya culture probably also resulted in an effective language shift" (Parpola 2008: 37). All speaks in favour of the warriors' capacity of potential – yet unpractised – intervention as the decisive factor which gave the early Indo-Europeans the edge for their successful takeover (Haarmann 2012: 95 ff.).

The Trypillya settlements, as a major regional complex of Old Europe, were interconnected, via trade routes, with the trade centers of the Danube civilization. These interconnections via trade attracted the pastoralists who, as migrants of the second out-migration from the steppe (Kurgan II), infiltrated parts of the region in the early centuries of the fourth millennium BCE. The pastoralists took influence and eventually also control.

Taking control over the settlements of agriculturalists as the result of destruction would not have made any sense since control over the lucrative trade market was the objective. That could be easily achieved by the show of force which the pastoralists had at their disposal: the warrior caste under the command of a local clan chief. The warrior caste was an institution that had originated already under the auspices of pastoralist life ways, characterized by a hierarchical social order (Haarmann and LaBGC 2021: 44 ff.).

This case may serve as a prototype model to understand the change brought about by immigrating groups of pastoralists. But it obviously became less popular during consecutive migrations (Kurgan II and III during the fourth and third millennia BCE) when the warriors engaged in open conflict with locals. Such conflicts speeded up the processes of spread of Indo-European groups throughout Europe. Warrior elites paved the way for ordinary migrants to follow (map 4).

Map 4: Out-migrations of steppe pastoralists (Kurgan II and III)

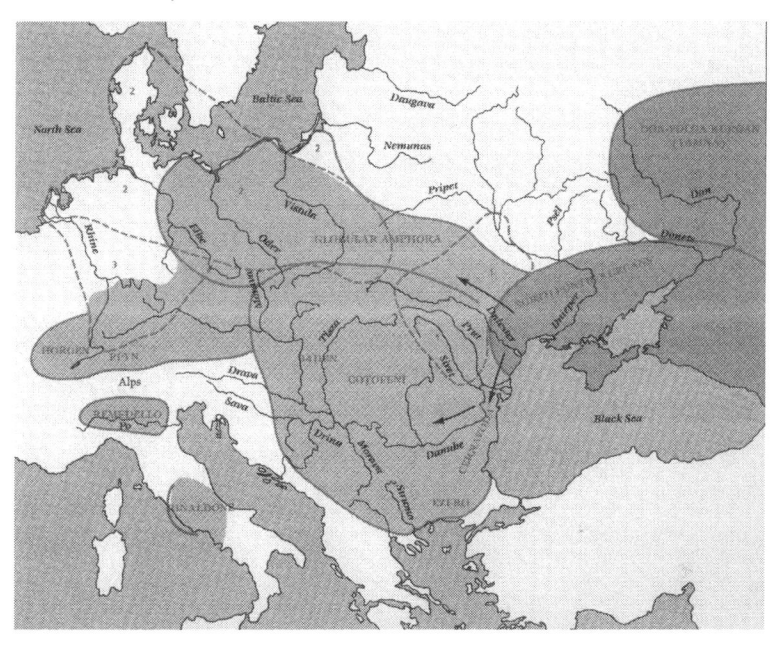

(fourth and third millennia BCE; Gimbutas 1991: 368)

– The significance of the interlude between the end of the second out-migration (Kurgan II) and the beginning of the third out-migration (Kurgan III)

On the eastern periphery of Old Europe, interactions intensified when newcomers (Indo-European pastoralists) and locals (ancient European agriculturalists) eventually came to terms and may have established even co-habitats. The pastoralists gradually experienced a shift to sedentary lifeways. Animal husbandry transformed to become a form of subsistence, as an addition to plant cultivation. The "agrarian package" was gradually adopted by the former pastoralists who kept up their contacts with kin folks in the steppe. What emerged was a milieu where members of the new elite and locals organized daily life under the auspices of biculturalism and bilingualism. The assumption has been made that the local inhabitants of the settlements "largely assimilated linguistically" (Parpola 2012: 127).

The region where bicultural interaction unfolded offered exceptional conditions for cooperation between the newcomers and the locals. It was in the northeastern part of Old Europe where the earliest megasettlements (or proto-cities) emerged, with thousands of inhabitants. In western Ukraine, truly large cities made their appearance, and these are known by the names of their respective archaeological sites: Majdanec'ke, Dobrovody and Tallyanky (map 5).

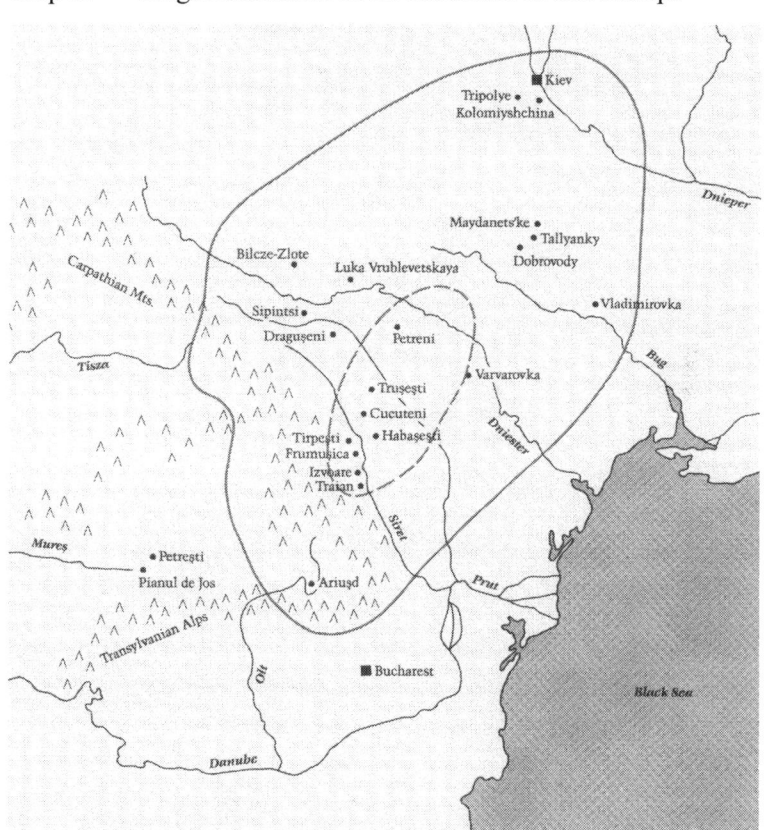

Map 5:   Megasettlements in the northeast of Old Europe

(fourth millennium BCE; Gimbutas 1991: 103 f.)

These metropolises were located northeast of the Bug river. The number of houses in these cities varied between 1,500 and 2,000. The largest of these Old European cities, Tallyanky, had an oval layout. The residential area was 3.5 km long and 1.5 km wide. An estimated 10,000 or more people lived there. The metropolis Majdanec'ke, with its 7,500 inhabitants, had an oval layout (Videjko 2005: 14). According to computer projections, the cultivated fields around these megasettlements must have extended up to 7 km into the surrounding area (Gaydarska 2003).

Those were the places where the most skilful metal-workers and craftsmen could be found. And it was in the milieu of the prosperous settlements with their high standards of technical know-how where the revolution of transport technology started out. The conditions of interaction of agriculturalists and pastoralists provided possibilities for technically skilled craftsmen to engage in joint ventures for achieving a breakthrough.

– The timespan for experimenting with transport technology

The time window for the origins of wheeled vehicles opens at the turn from the fifth to the fourth millennium BCE.

> "Between 4000 and 3400 BCE, the Late Tripolye [Trypillya] culture was the most thriving and populous agricultural community in the Copper Age world, cultivating extremely fertile black soil, and having villages that measured hundreds of hectares and that housed up to 15,000 people." (Parpola 2012: 126)

The period when pastoralists and agriculturalists interacted in the area of the Trypillya culture was characterized by stability of living-conditions. The second out-migration had ended around 3800 BCE and the third out-migration started around 3200 BCE. That gave community-life a peaceful span of development that lasted for several centuries.

The oldest archaeological finds of remnants of wheeled vehicles come from the area of intensive interaction between pastoralists and agriculturalists under the auspices of bicultural social life (Kuz'mina 2008: 135). Attempts have been made to reconstruct the outer appearance of the oldest wagon model, made of wood. That model had four wheels, made of solid disk-shaped plates (figure 9).

Figure 9: Reconstruction of the oldest model of a four-wheeled wagon

(Videjko 2008: 80)

The material for the disks for the wheels, hard wood, was provided by the forests bordering the lands used for plant cultivation.

– The creation of a specialized terminology of Indo-European coinage

Since pastoralists had established themselves as the elite, it seems conclusive that the specialized vocabulary for wheeled vehicles would be coined on the basis of the language of those in control. The predominance of the elite language is reflected in the Indo-European roots which have been analyzed in the documentations by David Anthony (1995) and Asko Parpola (2008, 2012); (figure 10).

Figure 10: The persistence of original terminology of wheel and wagon in the branches of the Indo-European phylum

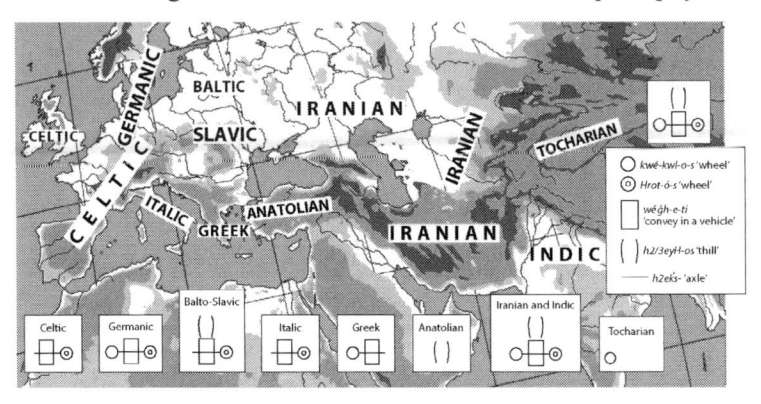

(Anthony and Ringe 2015: 204; courtesy of the authors)

The old layer of terminology relating to wheeled vehicles is comprised of Proto-Indo-European root words. In the inventory of terms there are no lexical borrowings from Sumerian. Such borrowings would exist had transport technology been invented in Mesopotamia in the early fourth millennium BCE. Since no such influx can be identified the alternative remains valid that the steppe pastoralists experimented with transport technology, in a joint venture of cooperation with the local agriculturalists in the megasettlements. In the process of coining specialized terminology, the language of the Indo-European elite was given priority.

> "The hypothesis that the wheeled vehicles were invented in the Tripolye culture [Late Tripolye thriving between 4000 and 3400 BCE in western Ukraine] after it had been taken over by PIE [Proto-Indo-European] speakers [...], gives a

satisfactory explanation to the puzzling question [...] where did the PIE get its vehicle terminology from." (Parpola 2012: 127)

Sidebar:

Key terms of wheeled vehicles with Proto-Indo-European roots

*kwekwlos	>	Greek kyklos "circle", Old Norse hvel "wheel", Old English hweohl "wheel", Old Indic cakrá "wheel, Sun disc", etc.
*rot-eh	>	Old Irish roth "wheel", Latin rota "wheel", Albanian rreth "ring; carriage tire", Old Indic rátha "wagon", etc.
*aks	>	Latin axis "axle, axis", Old English eax "axle", Mycenaean Greek (Linear B) a-ko-so-ne "axle", Old Indic áksa "axle", etc.
*wégheti	>	Latin veho "bear, convey", Old High German wegan "move, weigh", Old Indic váhati "transports, carries, conveys"; derivative nouns with the meaning "wagon" in Greek, Old Irish, Old Norse etc.
		(Anthony 2007: 35, 36, Mallory and Adams 2006: 247)

End of sidebar

– Conditions for migration facilitated by the introduction of wheel and wagon (Kurgan III)

The spread of transport technology and the related Indo-European terminology can be considered a leitmotif when tracing the movements of groups with Indo-European affiliation during the third out-migration (Kurgan III). News about the invention of wheeled vehicles spread rapidly into western regions. Already before the beginning of the third out-migration (starting around 3200 BCE) knowledge of the existence of wagons was transferred to the area of what is nowadays Bronocice in southern Poland. Archaeological excavations brought to light a sherd with the schematic depiction of a four-wheeled wagon, dating to c. 3400 BCE. This is the oldest visual evidence for a vehicle on wheels.

The incentive for innovation of transport technology was well motivated on both sides, among pastoralists as much as among agriculturalists although the advantages differ in sedentary communities from those in groups of mobile nomads.

The introduction of wheeled wagons in the agricultural communities facilitated the transfer of cargo and of people between the homestead and the fields. "Although the earliest wagons were slow and clumsy, […], they permitted single families to carry manure out to the fields and to bring firewood, supplies, crops, and people back home" (Anthony 2007: 72)

More varified were the advantages for the people from the steppe to which wheeled vehicles offered new possibilities for the movement of cargo. The use of pack animals required special efforts since the cargo had to be unloaded in the evening to give the animals a chance to rest overnight and, in the morning, the cargo had to be uploaded again. Once the wheeled wagon was in use, the cargo could remain in place for days without the need to be uploaded and unloaded in intervals. In addition, things could be transported in great amount.

"Wagons were useful in a different way in the open grasslands of the steppe, where the economy depended more on herding than on agriculture. Here wagons made portable things that had never been portable in bulk – shelter, water, and food." (Anthony 2007: 72 f.)

The chronological horizon of the spread of transport technology and its Indo-European terminology coincides with the archaeological evidence for the third out-migration (Kurgan III). As an epicenter of that movement, the contact area where pastoralists and agriculturalists cooperated on their joint venture of transport technology plays a pivotal role. The location of the Late Trypillya [Tripolye] culture (about 30° longitude and 50° latitude) is about the „centre of gravity" from where Indo-European languages spread west and east (Mallory 1989: 153).

"[…] when the Late Tripolye culture actually dissolved in the terminal C2 phase (c. 3400-2900 BCE), it gave way not only to local Post-Tripolye cultures but also created new cultures all around that share basic components of Tripolye and steppe origin. And these new cultures spread to those very regions where the various Indo-European languages first make their appearance, or, as in the case of Indo-Iranian, a good way along the route leading to those appearances." (Parpola 2012: 127 f.)

The epicenter of Indo-European dispersals has been identified by recent findings in human genetics (Haak et al. 2015), reconfirmed by further genetic analysis of aDNA for tracing the trails of pastoralists moving into southeastern and central Europe (Reich 2018).

– The input of ancient European technology and the fabric of ancient European terminology

In the megasettlements on the eastern fringe of Old Europe where contact conditions favoured the establishment of interethnic social relations and provided the incentive for cooperation in the technical fields, transport technology proliferated in two major branches. The Proto-Indo-European vocabulary of wheel and wagon testifies to the dominance of the language of the elite. And yet, there is another layer of equally old terminology, but these technical terms are unrelated to Indo-European. They are not of foreign origin, that is they are neither Sumerian nor Anatolian or Semitic. These terms are indigenous. Their ultimate source is the language of the ancient Europeans that left an imprint on later Greek civilization.

The archaeological record in the contact area does not give any clues where the workshops might have been, where ancient Europeans and former steppe pastoralists collaborated to improve transport technology. This means that the places where collaboration might have produced practical results cannot be identified.

What can be demonstrated is the persistence of a non-Indo-European set of specialized terms in ancient Greek. These terms, illustrating technical experiments among ancient Europeans, can be identified, as remnants, in the oldest layer of borrowed vocabulary of ancient Greek (Haarmann 2020: 93).

Sidebar:

Key terms of wheeled vehicles with ancient European roots

(i)	Terminology referring to four-wheeled wagon	
	amanan/amaxan	"chassis, wagon (with four wheels)"
	amaxa	"framework, chassis for a four-wheeled wagon; wagon"
	ampux	"rim of a wheel" ("If we analyse the word as *amp-uk-, it contains a typical substrate suffix" Beekes 2010: 92)
	apene	"four-wheeled wagon (synonymous with amaxa)"
(ii)	Terminology referring to two-wheeled cart	
	kapana / kapane	Thessalian word for 'wagon' (see apene)
	lampene / lapine	"a covered wagon (Thessalien)"
	morgos	"twined basket of a two-wheeled cart, in which straw and chaff was transported"
	othiza	"wagon drawn by mules"
	satinai	deriv. satilla "coach, carriage for women, equipage"
	smyliche	"the hole in the yoke in which the carriage pole is fixed"

End of sidebar

Apparently, the ancestors of the Greeks who had migrated into southeastern Europe from the steppe region carried two divergent sets of transport terminology in their cultural baggage when they occupied what was later called Hellas. The fact that elements of the ancient (= non-Indo-European) set of terms survived in ancient Greek may be due to the favourable conditions of lexical preservation in a language with its long-standing literary tradition, with beginnings dating to the seventeenth century BCE in the Mycenaean era. Several of the pre-Greek borrowings are documented in Linear B inscriptions.

– Conclusion

In the course of the Bronze Age, the migration of Indo-Europeans had infiltrated into most of southeastern Europe and came to dominate the major areas of Old Europe (Gimbutas 1991: 351 ff., Anthony 2007: 225 ff., Haarmann 2012: 87 ff.). By then the Old European cooperative society following the principle of gender equality in all aspects of community life was syncretizised by the Indo-European culture of hierarchy and patriarchy and possession orientated values which had caused parts of the indigenous population to leave their ancestral territory and migrate to regions not yet infiltrated and transformed by Indo-Europeans. The changes in settlement structures and demography caused by migratory movements and violent incursions were chaotic and produced something of a "dark age" (Mallory 1989: 238) in southeastern Europe.

Yet, the traditions from the old era were not eradicated completely. Under Indo-European aegis some traditions continued, experiencing transformations in the fusion processes and, already around 3500 BCE, the cultural exchange shows unmistakable results: "[…] an amalgamation of the Old European and Kurgan cultural systems is clearly evident" (Gimbutas 1991: 371).

Epilog: Mission to finally integrate Old Europe into historiography

A civilization that became the hub of such a stunningly wide range of fundamental first achievements like Old Europe did not vanish from the reality course of world history. Cultural features and technological items persisted in the fusion processes of subsequent societies and that mark the Old European heritage to our own time.

The mainstream of continuity has been mapped out in the foregoing, highlighting the great diversity of cultural patterns that persisted. Ancient Greek civilization is of paramount significance as a nodal point in the chronological sequence of continuity, and this for two reasons. The cultural fabric which makes up the Greek civilization originated in the course of the third and second millennia BCE which means that the formation of this civilization absorbed on a broad scale much of the fusion process of Old European and Indo-European features at an early date.

Recall that ancient Greek is the oldest literary language in Europe which means that much of the old heritage has been recorded in writing – starting around 1600 BCE – to support cultural memory. Secondly, what concerns the influence that Greek civilization had on other advanced cultures, the stamp of Greek antiquity with its imprints of much older patterns is at the very core of western civilization.

Evidence from DNA studies underscores the reality that, in the blood of modern Europeans, is encoded the gene profile of the ancient European (indigenous) population, that is of those people who developed and built up community life in Old Europe. This invisible heritage is combined with the visible traces which this early civilization left in subsequent cultures and in the canon of western civilization.

> "Wars, crises, short periods of peace. Why is it so difficult to bring to the lessons of the history of mankind, crystallized in more than 3000 uninterrupted peaceful years in ancient Europe? Just because the canon of our school education presents classical Greece as the cradle of our basic West ern values and the previous is still ignored?" (Haarmann & LaBGC 2022).

We have to take notice of the rich heritage of Old Europe and become conscious of its outstanding achievements. Old Europe is part of world history. And we repeat from our introduction: It is high time to correct outdated knowledge, to disseminate the valid findings about the first advanced civilization of mankind, its marks in subsequent cultures with influence to our time in words and images and eventually, bring the related historiography up to date. A cross media initiative is necessary from documentations – TV and podcasts – broadcasted via the internet, articles in newspapers and magazines, publications in school books and books of popular literature in order to bolster cultural awareness and to trigger action orientated at the Common Good and equality and opt insistently for a socially and environmentally lifestyle in which everyone has their place and task, is seen with respect and appreciation and thus is motivated to contribute to the whole knowing that what is achieved is the success of all.

The great fundamental research of Marija Gimbutas opened the view onto our Old European heritage. The contours drawn by her have been accentuated and broadened to be followed up. May science, in interdisciplinary cooperation, continue to investigate the millennia-long survival of the first advanced civilization as well as its gradual overforming by the Indo-European culture. We have to find a way forward to an again peaceful, prosperous togetherness.

WAKE UP

Marija Gimbutas in an interview with the
Los Angeles Times, 1989:

"Weapons, weapons, weapons! It's just incredible how many thousands of pounds of these daggers and swords were found from the Bronze Age. This was a cruel period and the beginning of what it is today - you turn on the television, and it's war, war, war, whatever channel."

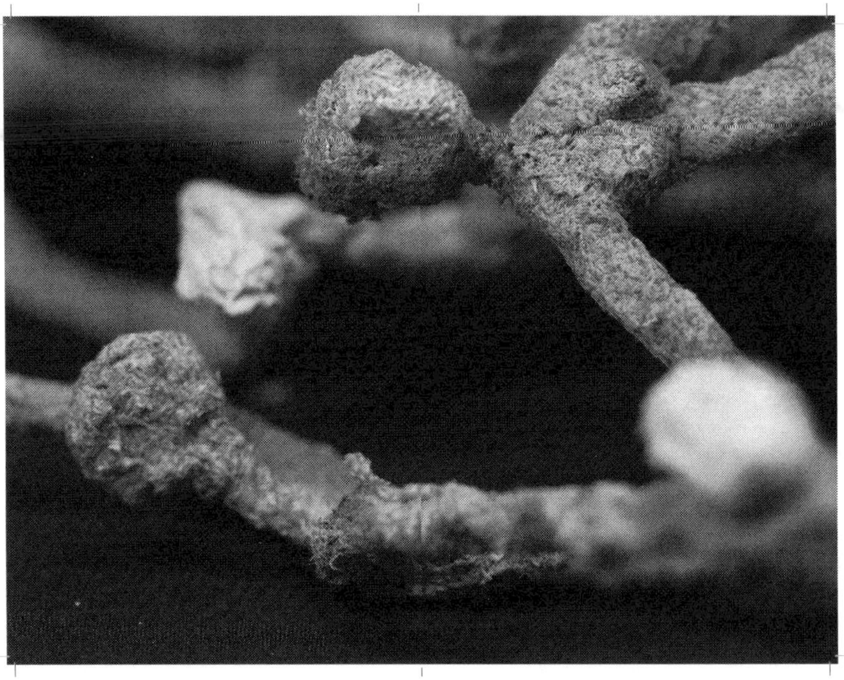

Joseph Campbell in his foreword to Marija Gimbutas'
The Language of the Goddess, 1989:

"One cannot but feel that in the appearance of this
volume at just this turn of the century there is an
evident relevance to the universally recognized
need in our time for a general transformation of
consciousness. The message here is of an actual
age of harmony and peace in accord with the
creative energies of nature which for the spell of
some four thousand prehistoric years anteceded
the five thousand of what James Joyce has termed
the 'nightmare' (of contending tribal and national
interests) from which it is now certainly time for
this planet to wake."

> When are we going to wake up?
> **KNOW ACT NOW**

LaBCE 2021

Bibliography

Anderson, D.E. et al. (2007). Global environments through the quaternary. Exploring environmental change. Oxford.

Alcock, Susan E., and Robin Osborne (eds.) (1994). Placing the gods: Sanctuaries and sacred space in ancient Greece. Oxford & New York: Clarendon Press.

Anthony, David (1995). "Horse, wagon and chariot: Indo-European languages and archaeology." Antiquity 69: 554-565.

Anthony, David et al. (2022). "The Eneolithic cemetery at Khvalynsk on the Volga river." Prähistorische Zeitschrift (online publication); (Paper / doi.org/10.1515/pz-2022-2034).

Anthony, David and Don Ringe (2015). "The Indo-European homeland from linguistic and archaeological perspectives." Annual Review of Linguistics 1: 199-219.

Anthony, David W. (2007). The horse, the wheel and language: How Bronze-Age riders from the Eurasian steppes shaped the modern world. Princeton, New Jersey & Oxford: Princeton University Press.

– (ed.) (2010). The lost world of Old Europe. The Danube valley, 5000 – 3500 BC. Princeton, New Jersey & Oxford: Princeton University Press.

– (2007). The horse, the wheel and language. How Bronze-Age riders from the Eurasian steppes shaped the modern world. Princeton & Oxford.

– (2009a). The rise and fall of Old Europe, in: Anthony 2009b: 28-57.

– (ed.) (2009b). The lost world of Old Europe – The Danube valley 5000 – 3500 BC. Princeton, New Jersey & Oxford.

Antonaccio, Carla M. (1994). "Placing the past: The Bronze Age in the cultic topography of early Greece." In Alcock and Osborne 1994: 79-104.

Arena, Renato (1996). "The Greek colonization of the West: Dialects." In Pugliese Carratelli 1996: 189-200.

Auffarth, Christoph (2010). "The materiality of god's image: The Olympian Zeus and ancient christology." In Bremmer and Erskine 2010: 465-480.

Bachvarov, K. and Glesner, R. (eds.) (2016). Southeast Europe and Anatolia in prehistory: Essays in honor of Vassil Nikolov on his 65th anniversary. Bonn: Verlag Dr. Rudolf Habelt.

Bădocan, I. (2007). "Gesturi sacre și profane la întermeierea familiei." Anuarul Muzeului Etnografic al Transilvaniei 2007: 299-305.

Bammesberger, Alfred and Theo Vennemann (eds.) (2004). Languages in prehistoric Europe. Heidelberg: Winter (2nd ed.).

Bar-Yosif, O. (2017). "Multiple origins of agriculture in Eurasia and Africa." In Tibayrenc and Ayala 2017: 297-331.

Barile, Giuseppe (2019). Dialogue between stone men. An idea for Matera 2019 – European Capital of Culture. Irsina: Centro Studi – GIO: Maria Trabaci.

Barringer, Judith M. (2008). Art, myth, and ritual in classical Greece. Cambridge & New York: Cambridge University Press.

Barron, Lee (2014). Celebrity cultures: An introduction. Thousand Oaks, California: SAGE publications.

Beekes, Robert (2004). "Indo-European or substrate? Phatne and keryx." In Bammesberger and Vennemann 2004: 109-115.

– (2010). Etymological dictionary of Greek, 2 vols. Leiden & Boston: Brill.

– (2011). Comparative Indo-European linguistics: An Introduction. Amsterdam & Philadelphia, Pennsylvania: John Benjamins (2nd ed.).

Bilţiu, P. (2007). "Substratul mitico-magic al portii şi funcţiile ei în cultura populara maramureseană şi românească." Anuarul Muzeului Etnografic al Transilvaniei 2007: 243-259.

Bintliff, John (2011). The complete archaeology of Greece: From hunter-gatherers to the 20th century A.D. Malden, Massachusetts & Oxford: Wiley-Blackwell.

Blok, Josine H. (1995). The early Amazons. Modern & ancient perspectives on a persistent myth. Leiden, New York & Cologne: E.J. Brill.

Bomgardner, David Lee (2000). The story of the Roman amphitheatre: London & New York: Routledge.

Borić, Dušan (1999). "Places that created time in the Danube gorges and beyond, c. 9000-5500 BC." Documenta Praehistorica XXVI: 41-70.

Borzenkova, Irena Ivanova et al. (2015). Climate change during the Holocene (past 12,000 years). In The BACC II Author Team (eds.). Second assessment of climate change for the Baltic Sea Basin; pp. 25-49.

Bremmer, Jan N. (2010). "Introduction: The Greek gods in the twentieth century." In Bremmer and Erskine 2010: 1-18.

Bremmer, Jan N., and Andrew Erskine (eds.) (2010). The gods of ancient Greece: Identities and transformations. Edinburgh: Edinburgh University Press.

Brukner, Bogdan. (2002). „Die Vinča-Kultur in Raum und Zeit." Akademija Nauka i Umjetnosti Bosne i Hercegovine – Godisnjak 32: 61-103.

– (2006). "Possible influences of the Black Sea flood on the formation of Vinča culture." Journal of Archaeomythology 2: 17-26.

Bucur, Corneliu, Gangolea, Cornelia, Munteanu, Dan and Sedler, Irmgard (eds.) (1986). Museum of folk technology guide book. Sibiu: Direction of the Brukenthal Museum.

Budja, Mihael (2004). "The transition to farming and the 'revolution' of symbols in the Balkans. From ornament to entoptic and external symbolic storage." Documenta Praehistorica XXXI: 59-81.

– (2005). "The process of Neolithisation in South-eastern Europe: from ceramic female figurines and cereal grains to entoptics and human nuclear DNA polymorphic markers." Documenta Praehistorica XXXII (2005): 53-72.

Budja, M. (2007). "The 8200 calBP 'climate event' and the process of Neolithisation in south-eatsren Europe", in: Documenta Praehistorica 34: 191-201.

Burroughs, William J. (2005). Climate change in prehistory. The end of the reign of chaos. Cambridge & New York: Cambridge University Press.

Chave, Anna C. (1993). Constantin Brancusi. Shifting the bases of art. New Haven & London: Yale University Press.

Chwe, Michael Suk-Young (2001). Rational ritual: culture, coordination, and common knowledge. Princeton, New Jersey: Princeton University Press.

Cline, Eric H. (ed.) (2010). The Oxford handbook of the Bronze Age Aegean. Oxford & New York: Oxford University Press.

Conard, Nicholas J., Floss, Harald, Barth, Martina and Serangeli, Jordi (eds.) (2009). Eiszeit – Kunst und Kultur. Ostfildern: Thorbecke Verlag.

Connelly, Joan Breton (2014). The Parthenon enigma. A new understanding of the West's most iconic building and the people who made it. New York: Alfred A. Knopf.

Csapo, Eric and Margaret C. Miller (eds.) (2007). The origins of theatre in ancient Greece and beyond. Cambridge & New York: Cambridge University Press.

Cultraro, Massimo (2011). I Micenei: Archeologia, storia, società dei Greci prima di Omero. Rome: Carocci editore (5th ed.).

Danforth, L.M. (1982). The death rituals of rural Greece. Princeton, New Jersey: Princeton University Press.

Daniels, Peter T. and William Bright (eds.) (1996). The World's writing systems. New York & Oxford: Oxford University Press.

Davis, BAS et al. (2003). "The temperature of Europe during the Holocene reconstructed from pollen data". Quaternary Sci Rev 22: 1701-1716.

Deacon, Terrence (1997). The symbolic species. The co-evolution of language and the human brain. London: The Penguin Press.

Deacy, Susan (2001). Athena in the classical world. Leiden: Brill.

–   (2008). Athena. London & New York: Routledge.

Dickinson, Oliver (1994). The Aegean Bronze Age. Cambridge & New York: Cambridge University Press.

Doumas, Christos (1992). The wall-paintings of Thera. Athens: The Thera Foundation – Petros M. Nomikos.

Everson, Stephen (ed.) (1991). Companions to ancient thought 2: Psychology. Cambridge: Cambridge University Press.

Faulkner, Neil (2012). A visitor's guide to the ancient Olympics. New Haven & London: Yale University Press.

Gaydarska, B. (2003). „Application of GIS in settlement archaeology: An integrated approach to prehistoric subsistence strategies." In Korvin-Piotorvsky et al. 2003: 212-216.

Gheorghiu, D. and R. Skeates (eds.) (2008). Prehistoric stamps – Theory and experiments. Bukarest: Editura universitatii din București.

Gimbutas, Marija (1989). The language of the Goddess. San Francisco: Harper & Row.

– (1991). The Civilization of the Goddess: The World of Old Europe. San Francisco: Harper Collins.

Gogos, Savas (2008). Das Dionysostheater von Athen: Architektonische Gestalt und Funktion. Vienna: Phoibos.

Gombrich, Ernst (1960). Art and Illusion: A study in the psychology of pictorial representation. Princeton, NJ: Princeton University Press.

Gould, Richard A. (2011). Archaeology and the social history of ships. Cambridge & New York: Cambridge University Press (2nd ed.).

Graf, Fritz (1993). Greek mythology – An introduction. Baltimore & London: Johns Hopkins University Press.

Graziosi, Barbara (2002). Inventing Homer: The early reception of epic. Cambridge: Cambridge University Press.

Grünthal, Riho and Petri Kallio (eds.) (2012). A linguistic map of prehistoric northern Europe: Helsinki: Société Finno-Ougrienne.

Haak, W. et al. (2015). Massive migration from the steppe was a source for Indo-European languages in Europe, in: Nature 522: 207-211; Nature 14317. http://www.nature.com/nature/journal/vaop/ncurrent/pdf/nature14317.pdf.

Haarmann, Harald (1995). Early civilization and literacy in Europe. An inquiry into cultural continuity in the Mediterranean world. Berlin & New York: Mouton de Gruyter.

Haarmann, Harald (2003). Geschichte der Sintflut. Auf den Spuren der frühen Zivilisationen. Munich: C.H. Beck (3rd ed. 2015), (4rd ed. 2022).

— (2007). Foundations of culture. Knowledge-construction, belief systems and worldview in their dynamic interplay. Frankfurt, Berlin & New York: Peter Lang.

— (2008). "A comparative view of the Danube script and other ancient writing systems." In Marler 2008: 11-22.

— (2009). Interacting with figurines: Seven dimensions in the study of imagery. West Hartford, Vermont: Full Circle Press.

— (2010a). Einführung in die Donauschrift. Hamburg: Buske.

— (2011). Das Rätsel der Donauzivilisation. Die Entdeckung der ältesten Hochkultur Europas. Munich: C.H. Beck (3rd ed. 2017).

— (2012). Indo-Europeanization – day one. Elite recruitment and the beginnings of language politics. Wiesbaden: Harrassowitz.

— (2013a). Ancient knowledge, ancient know-how, ancient reasoning. Cultural memory in transition from prehistory to classical antiquity and beyond. Amherst, New York: Cambria.

— (2013b). "Language and ethnicity in antiquity." In McInerney 2013: 17-33.

– (2014). Roots of ancient Greek civilization. The influence of Old Europe. Jefferson, North Carolina: McFarland.

– (2017). Plato's philosophy reaching beyond the limits of reason. Contours of a contextual theory of truth. Hildesheim, Zurich & New York: Olms.

– (2018). "Who taught the ancient Greeks the craft of shipbuilding? On the pre-Greek roots of maritime technological know-how". Mankind Quarterly 59: 155-170.

– (2019a). The mystery of the Danube civilisation. The discovery of Europe's oldest civilisation. Wiesbaden: Verlagshaus Römerweg.

– (2019b). Plato's sophia. His philosophical endeavor in light of its spiritual currents and undercurrents. Amherst, New York: Cambria.

– (2019c). Die Anfänge Roms. Geschichte einer Mosaikkultur. Wiesbaden: Verlagshaus Römerweg.

– (2020). On the trail of the Indo-Europeans. From Neolithic steppe nomads to early civilisations. Wiesbaden: marixverlag.

– (2020a). Advancement in ancient civilizations. Life, culture, science and thought. Jefferson, North Carolina: McFarland.

– (2020b). Platons Musen – Philosophie im Licht weiblicher Intellektualität. Hildesheim, Zurich & New York: Olms.

– (2022). Die Erfindung des Rades – Die frühen Hochkulturen im Spiegel einer bahnbrechenden Innovation. Munich: C.H. Beck (forthcoming).

Haarmann, Harald and Joan Marler (2008). Introducing the Mythological Crescent: Ancient beliefs and imagery connecting Eurasia with Anatolia. Wiesbaden: Harrassowitz.

Haarmann, Harald and LaBGC (2021). The hero cult. A spectacle of world history that changed civilization. Wiesbaden: Harrassowitz.

- (2022). Europäisches Selbstverständnis im Umbruch – Eine neue Entstehungsgeschichte unserer Grundwerte. Basel & Nürnberg: Seubert Verlag.

Haarmann, Harald and Joan Marler (2021). "Marija Gimbutas – A visionary's legacy" In Journal of Archaeomythology 10: 9-21.

Hall, Edith (2014). Introducing the ancient Greeks. From Bronze Age seafarers to navigators of the western mind. New York & London: W.W. Norton & Company.

Hall, Jonathan M. (2002). Hellenicity between ethnicity and culture. Chicago & London: The University of Chicago Press.

Howatson, M.C. (ed.) (2011). The Oxford companion to classical literature. Oxford & New York: Oxford University Press (3rd ed.).

Hunter, Richard and Ian Rutherford (2009a). „Introduction." In Hunter and Rutherford 2009b: 1-22.

– (eds.) (2009b). Wandering poets in ancient Greek culture. Travel, locality and pan-Hellenism. Cambridge: Cambridge University Press.

Hurwit, Jeffrey M. (2000). The Athenian Acropolis: History, mythology, and archaeology from the Neolithic era to the present. Cambridge: Cambridge University Press.

Ilieva, A. and A. Shturbanova (1997). "Zoomorphic images in Bulgarian women's ritual dances in the context of Old European symbolism." In Marler 1997: 309-321.

Ilievski, Petar Chr. (2000). Zhivotot na mikencite vo nivnite pismeni svedoshtva, so poseben osvrt kon onomastickite i prosopografski izvodi (The life of the Mycenaeans from their own records, with special regard to the onomastic and prosopographic deductions). Skopje: Makedonska Akademija na Naukite i Umetnostite.

Ingold, Tim (ed.) (1994). Companion encyclopedia of anthropology. Humanity, culture and social life. London & New York: Routledge.

Jeffery, L.H. (1990). The local scripts of archaic Greece: A study of the origins of the Greek alphabet and its development from the eighth to the fifth centuries B.C. Oxford: Oxford University Press (2nd ed.).

Jensen, Minna Skate (1980). The Homeric question and the oral formulaic theory. Copenhagen: Museum Tusculanum Press.

Jones, Eppie R. et al. (2015). Upper Palaeolithic genomes reveal deep roots of modern Eurasians. Nature Communications | 6:8912 | DOI: 10.1038/ncomms9912 | www.nature.com/nature communications.

Jones, Phil (1996). Drama as therapy. Theatre as living. London & New York: Routledge.

Jones-Bley, K., Huld, M.E., Volpe, A. della and M.R. Dexter (eds.) (2008). Proceedings of the 19th annual UCLA Indo-Europeanconference, Los Angeles, November 2-3, 2007, Washington, D.C.

Komitska, Anita, Borissova, Veska and Velislav Nikolov (2000). Bulgarian folk costumes. Sofia: Borina Pub House.

Korvin-Piotorvsky, A., Kruts, V., and S. Rizhov (eds.). (2003). Tripolye settlements-giants. Kiev.

Kowalzig, Barbara (2007). Singing for the gods. Oxford: Oxford University Press.

Kozlowski, Janusz K. (1992). L'Art de la Préhistoire en Europe Orientale Milan: Presses du CNRS.

Kruta, Venceslas (1993). Die Anfänge Europas 6000–500 v.Chr. Munich: C.H. Beck.

Kuz'mina, E.E. (2008). The prehistory of the Silk Road. Philadelphia.

LaBGC and Harald Haarmann (2019). Miteinander Neu-Denken. Europa im Gestern | Alteuropa im Heute [English version: Re-Thinking Togetherness, 2021]. Berlin: LIT Verlag.

— (2021). Re-Thinking togetherness. Know. act. now. Berlin: LIT Verlag.

Lape, Susan (2010). Race and citizen identity in the classical Athenian emocracy. Cambridge & New York: Cambridge University Press.

Lazaridis, Iosif et al. (2017). „Genetic origins of the Minoans and Mycenaeans." Nature 548: 214-218.

Liddell, Henry George and Robert Scott (1883). A Greek-English lexicon. New York: Harper & Brothers; Oxford: Clarendon Press (ninth edition, revised and augmented by Henry Stuart Jones, 1940; with revised supplement, printed 1991).

Majercik, Ruth (1989). The Chaldean Oracles: Text, translation and commentary. Leiden, Copenhagen & Cologne: Brill.

Mallory, J.P. (1989). In search of the Indo-Europeans: Language, archaeology and myth. London: Thames and Hudson.

Mallory, J.P. and D.Q. Adams (eds.) (1997). Encyclopedia of Indo-European culture. London & Chicago: Fitzroy Dearborn Publishers.

— (2006). The Oxford introduction to Proto-Indo-European and the Proto-Indo-European world. Oxford & New York: Oxford University Press.

Marinatos, Nanno (1993). Minoan religion: Ritual, image, and symbol. Columbia, South Carolina: University of South Carolina Press.

Marler, Joan (ed.) (1997). From the realm of the ancestors: An anthology in honor of Marija Gimbutas. Manchester, Connecticut: Knowledge, Ideas & Trends.

— (ed.) (2008). The Danube script. Neo-eneolithic writing in southeastern Europe. Sebastopol, CA: Institute of Archaeomythology.

Marler, Joan and Harald Haarmann (eds.) (2006). The Black Sea flood: An interdisciplinary investigation. Journal of Archaeomythology, volume 2. Sebastopol, California.

- (2022a). Marija Gimbutas' contributions to archaeology and the reactions within her field: Examining the backlash and reassessing her significance and legacy (Diss.). San Francisco: California Institute of Integral Studies.

- (2022b). "Baltic archaeology, cultural history, ancient Lithuanian symbolism, Old Europe, and the Archaeomythology of Marija Gimbutas" In Archaeologia Lituana 23:10-33.

Mastromarco, Giuseppe and Piero Totaro (2012). Storia del teatro greco. Milan: Mondadori (2nd ed.).

Mathieson, I. et al. (2018). "The genomic history of southeastern Europe." Nature 555: 197-203.

Maxim, Zoia, Marler, Joan and Viorica Crisan (eds.) (2009). The Danube script in light of the Turdaș and Tărtăria discoveries. Cluj-Napoca: National Museum of Transylvania.

McCarthy, E. Doyle (1996). Knowledge as culture: The new sociology of knowledge. London & New York: Routledge.

McInerney, Jeremy (ed.) (2013). A companion to ethnicity in the ancient Mediterranean. Oxford: Wiley-Blackwell.

Meillet, Antoine (1937). Introduction à l'étude comparative des langues indo-européennes. Paris: Hachette.

Merlini, Marco (2004). La scrittura è nata in Europa? Rome: Avverbi.

– (2009a). An inquiry into the Danube script. Sibiu & Alba Iulia: Editura Altip.

Michalopoulos, Dimitri (2016). Homer's Odyssey beyond the myths. The Piraeus: Institute of Hellenic Maritime History.

Miller, Dean A. (1997). "Warriors." In Mallory and Adams 1997: 631-636.

Miller, Sanda (2010). Constantin Brancusi. London: Reaktion Books.

Morpurgo Davies, Anna and Yves Duhoux (eds.) (1988). Linear B: a 1984 survey. Louvain-la-Neuve: Peeters.

Morris, S. and R. Laffineur (eds.) (2007). EPOS: Reconsidering Greek epic and Aegean Bronze Age archaeology. Austin: University of Texas Press.

Morrison, J.S. and R.T. Williams (1968). Greek oared ships 900 – 322 B.C. Cambridge: Cambridge University Press.

Naumov, G. (2008). "Neolithic stamps from the southern part of the Balkan Peninsula." In Gheorghiu and Skeates 2008: 43-84.

Nikolov, Vassil (ed.) (2008). Provadia-Solnitsata. Prehistoric salt-producing center. Sofia.

Oakley, John H. (2013). The Greek vase. Art of the storyteller. London: The British Museum Press.

Ober, Josiah (2008). Democracy and knowledge. Innovation and learning in classical Athens. Princeton, New Jersey & Oxford: Princeton University Press.

Osborne, Robin (1996). Greece in the making 1200 – 479 BC. London & New York: Routledge.

Owens, Garreth A. (1999). "Balkan Neolithic scripts." Kadmos 38: 114-120.

Parpola, Asko (2008). "Proto-Indo-European speakers of the late Tripolye culture as the inventors of wheeled vehicles: Linguistic and archaeological considerations of the PIE homeland problem", in: Jones-Bley et al. 2008: 1-59.

–   (2012). "Formation of the Indo-European and Uralic (Finno-Ugric) language families in the light of archaeology: Revised and integrated 'total' correlations." In Grünthal and Kallio 2012: 119-184.

Pelikan, J. (1996). Mary through the centuries. Her place in the history of culture. New Haven: Yale University Press.

Poruciuc, Adrian (1995). Archaeolinguistica: Tre studii interdisciplinare. Bukarest: Institutul Român de Tracologie.

–   (2010). Prehistoric roots of Romanian and Southeast European traditions. Sebastopol, California: Institute of Archaeomythology.

Pugliese Carratelli, Giovanni (ed.) (1996). The western Greeks. Classical civilization in the western Mediterranean. London: Thames and Hudson.

Radoane, Maria (2021). "A history of the circum-pontic river channels marked by climate and sea level changes during the Late Quaternary (25-8 ka BP)." Revista de Geomorfologie 23: 91-120.

Raduncheva, Ana (2003). Kasnoneolitnoto obshtestvo v balgarskite zemi. Sofia: The Bulgarian Academy of Sciences.

Reich, David (2018). Who We Are and How We Got Here: Ancient DNA and the New Science of the Human Past. New York: Pantheon.

Renfrew, Colin (1991). The Cycladic spirit. New York: Harry N. Abrams.

Roselli, David Kawalko (2011). Theater of the people. Spectators and society in ancient Athens. Austin: University of Texas Press.

Ruijgh, C.J. (1988). "Le mycénien et Homère." In Morpurgo Davies, and Duhoux 1988: 143-190.

Runnels, Curtis and Priscilla M. Murray (2001). Greece before history: An archaeological companion and guide. Stanford: Stanford University Press.

Ryan, William and Walter Pitman (1998). Noah's flood. The new scientific discoveries about the event that changed history. New York: Simon & Schuster.

Salway, Peter (1993). The Oxford illustrated history of Roman Britain. Oxford & New York: Oxford University Press.

Schechner, Richard (1994). "Ritual and performance." In Ingold 1994: 613-647.

Scheid, John and Jesper Svenbro (1996). The craft of Zeus. Cambridge, MA & London: Harvard University Press.

Schofield, M. (1991). "Heraclitus' theory of soul and its antecedents." In Everson 1991: 13-34.

Shearer, Ann (1996). Athene: Image and energy. London & New York: Viking Arkana.

Slavchev, Vladimir (2009). "The Varna Eneolithic cemetery in the context of the late Copper Age in the East Balkans". In Anthony 2009b: 192-210.

Smart, Ninian (1997). Dimensions of the sacred. An anatomy of the world's beliefs. London: Fontana Press.

Threatte, Leslie (1996). "The Greek alphabet." In Daniels and Bright 1996: 271-280.

Tibayrenc, Michel and Francisco J. Ayala (eds.). On human nature. Biology, psychology, ethics, politics, and religion. Amsterdam, Heidelberg, London & New York: Elsevier.

Turner, John D. (2010). "The Chaldean Oracles and the metaphysics of the Sethian Platonizing Treatises." In Turner and Corrigan 2010: 213-232.

Turner, John D. and Kevin Corrigan (eds.) (2010). Plato's Parmenides and its heritage, vol. 1: History and interpretation from the Old Academy to later Platonism and Gnosticism. Atlanta, Georgia: Society of Biblical Literature.

Tzonou-Herbst, Ioulia (2010). "Figurines." Cline 2010: 210-222.

Varia, Radu (1986). Brancusi. New York: Rizzoli International Publications.

Vasileva, Margarita (ed.) (2003). Traditional Bulgarian calendar – Illustrated encyclopedia. Plovdiv: Bulgarian Academy of Sciences.

Vassányi, Miklós (2011). Anima mundi: The rise of the world soul theory in modern German philosophy. Dordrecht, Heidelberg, London & New York: Springer.

Vernant, Jean-Pierre and Pierre Vidal-Naquet (1990). Myth and tragedy in ancient Greece. New York: Zone Books.

Videiko, M. J. (2003). Trypil´s´ka tsivilizatsiia. Kiev (2nd ed.).

– (2008). Ukraina: Ot Tripol'ia do Antov. Kiev.

Wachter, Rudolf (1989). „Zur Vorgeschichte des griechischen Alphabets." Kadmos 28: 19-78.

Waller, D. (2010). Textiles from the Balkans. London: British Museum Press.

Watrous, L.V. (2007). "The fleet fresco, the Odyssey and Greek epic narrative." In Morris and Laffineur 2007: 97-105.

Werner, Daniel S. (2012). Myth and philosophy in Plato's Phaedrus. Cambridge & New York: Cambridge University Press.

Wiles, David (1997). Tragedy in Athens. Performance space and theatrical meaning. Cambridge & New York: Cambridge University Press.

Wilson, Stephen (1998). The means of naming: A social and cultural history of personal naming in western Europe. London & Bristol: UCL Press.

Winn, Shan M.M. (1981). Pre-writing in Southeastern Europe: The sign system of the Vinča culture ca. 4000 B.C. Calgary: Western Publishers.

Yakar, Jak (2016). "The nature and extent of Neolithic Anatolia's contribution to the emergence of farming communities in the Balkans – an overview." In Bachvarov and Glesner 2016: 25-68.

Yanko-Hombach, Valentina et al. (eds.) (2007). The Black Sea flood question: Changes in coastline, climate and human settlement. Heidelberg: Springer.

Yasumura, Noriko (2011). Challenges to the power of Zeus in early Greek poetry. London: Bristol Classical Press.

List of maps and figures

Maps

Map 1: The network of local and interregional trade routes inside and outside the core area of Old Europe (Haarmann 2020a: 62)

Map 2: Sites with finds of inscriptions in the cultural provinces of the Danube civilization (irradiation centers for the use of writing are bordered; Merlini 2004, fig. II, with additions)

Map 3: Varna and its hinterland in the fifth millennium BCE (Gimbutas 1991: 92)

Map 4: Out-migrations of steppe pastoralists (Kurgan II and III) (fourth and third millennia BCE; Gimbutas 1991: 368)

Map 5: Megasettlements in the northeast of Old Europe (fourth millennium BCE; Gimbutas 1991: 103 f.)

Figures

Figure 1: The continuation of Old European leitmotifs in the Bronze Age (third millennium BCE)

    a) A figurine from Lerna

(Runnels and Murray 2001: 58)

    b) Clay seals with linear signs from Lerna

(Dickinson 1994: 190)

Figure 2: Hera suckling Herakles (red-figure vase, c. 370 BCE; Oakley 2013: 64)

Figure 3: A female runner at the Heraia of Olympia (bronze figurine, c. 500 BCE; courtesy of The British Museum)

Figure 4: Sculptures from the regional Neolithic culture of Hamangia (Cernavoda, Romania; ca. 4800 BCE); (Kruta 1993: 84, 85)

Figure 5: Signs on a spherical stone from Lepenski Vir (Winn 1981: 259)

Figure 6: Sign inventory of the Danube script (selection)

    a) Iconic signs

    b) Abstract signs

(Haarmann 1995, fig. 32)

Figure 7: The supplementary letters of the Greek alphabet and their equivalents in Aegean linear writing (Haarmann 1995, fig. 170 and 171)

Figure 8: Copper axes from the Varna Necropolis (Slavchev 2009: 201)

Figure 9: Reconstruction of the oldest model of a four-wheeled wagon (Videjko 2008: 80)

Figure 10: The persistence of original terminology of wheel and wagon in the branches of the Indo-European phylum (Anthony and Ringe 2015: 204; courtesy of the authors)

Harald Haarmann, a German linguist and cultural philosopher and resident of Finnland; Vice President of the Institute of Archaeomythology and Director of its European Branch; his research has for many years focused on Old Europe as the cradle of the basic values of the Western civilization.

LaBGC, an artist and publicist living in Spain; she is interested in egalitarian forms of society with a peaceful orientation, which motivated her to collaborate with Harald Haarmann; together they have written several books in German and English.

Bibliographic Information of the German National Library. The German National Library registers this publication in the German National Bibliography; detailed bibliographic data on the Internet at http://d-nb.de.

All rights reserved. The work is protected by copyright. Any use beyond the limits of copyright is prohibited and punishable without the permission of the publisher. This applies in particular to duplications, translations, microfilming, storage and processing in electronic systems.

© Seubert Verlag Basel; Nuremberg 2023

Layout, cover and typesetting: Kristina Schippling

Cover picture: adaptation – Kristina Schippling; Sculptures from the regional Neolithic culture of Hamangia (Cernavoda, Romania; ca. 4800 BCE)

ISBN: 978-3-98795-019-3

Printed in Poland
by Amazon Fulfillment
Poland Sp. z o.o., Wrocław
13 August 2023

ef0a5a48-2177-40a4-8327-cbb2c7eaa0fbR01